Leon Chaitow is a Registered Osteopath and Naturopath, as well as an established author of books and articles on health-related issues. In heavy demand as a teacher of soft tissue manipulation at chiropractic and naturopathic colleges in both Europe and the United States, he is also editor of the *Journal of Alternative and Complementary Medicine* and a regular contributor to *Here's Health* magazine.

The Stress Protection Plan

How to stay healthy under pressure
Leon Chaitow N.D., D.O.

Thorsons
An Imprint of HarperCollins*Publishers*

Thorsons
An Imprint of HarperCollins*Publishers*
77-85 Fulham Palace Road
Hammersmith, London W6 8JB

First published as *Your Complete Stress-Proofing Programme* 1983

This completely revised and expanded
edition published 1992

10 9 8 7 6 5 4 3 2 1

© Leon Chaitow 1983, 1992

Leon Chaitow asserts the moral right to
be identified as the author of this work

A catalogue record for this book
is available from the British Library

ISBN 0 7225 2501 X

Typeset by Harper Phototypesetters Limited,
Northampton, England
Printed in Great Britain by
HarperCollinsManufacturing Glasgow

Contents

Acknowledgements

In the text, reference is made to numerous researchers and writers whose work I have distilled into the sections on the treatment of stress. I wish to express my gratitude to all of these people. In particular, I would like to record my gratitude to the late Bagnell Goodwin, who first kindled my interest in the importance of 'stress-proofing' when I was a student at the British College of Naturopathy and Osteopathy between 1956 and 1960.

To my darling wife, Alkmini,
a counsellor of rare skill from
whom I have learned much.

INTRODUCTION

Choosing to Become Less Stressed

There will always be stress in life, and really what we have to look at is our reaction to it rather than trying to make the stress go away. In this book I explain a number of practical ways to enable you to better cope with the pressures you find yourself under.

But, first, let us look at exactly what stress is, since once you have understood the diverse nature of it, and its possible ramifications in terms of ill health, you will more readily be able to see the importance of these stress-management methods.

Where applicable wrist watches used to be described as 'waterproof', but this expression now tends to be altered to 'water resistant'. In stating the degree of resistance the manufacturers have, of course, to take into account the nature of the hazard and the properties and quality of the instrument, as well as the different sorts of water it might be immersed in (salt water, fresh water, acid or alkaline water etc.), and the depths beyond which its resistance begins to deteriorate. There are other hazards, too, facing wrist watches, such as shock, heat, cold, magnetic fields and so on.

In the same way we face a range of stress factors, and it is not possible to 'stress-proof' ourselves absolutely. Stress resistance can be increased, however, and as in the case of the watch, we have to look at the variable stress factors and the nature of the instrument at risk – that is, you. The aim is, therefore, not to try to eliminate stress, but to modify it where possible and to encourage in yourself appropriate responses to it.

Variables exist not only in the nature and intensity of the stress you face, but also in the unique characteristics which each of us possess. Some of us are born with a strong degree of what is termed 'hardiness', whilst others seem to be short of this innate defensive shield.

The hardiness factor is a combination of things, including a sense of being in *control* of life and events, a feeling that the multiple changes which occur throughout life present *challenges* or opportunities rather than threats, and a wish to be involved in society and the lives of others (*commitment*). The good news is that, as with so many aspects of stress-proofing, these positive, stress-coping characteristics can be learned and acquired once you know more about them.

The whole subject of hardiness, as well as the importance of understanding the role of happiness and cynicism in your life and their effects on your health, are fully explained in Chapter 4.

The state of your health is the result of the complex interrelationship between the uniqueness of you and the challenges and stresses of your particular internal and external environment. Those stresses can be self-produced (e.g. anger, fear) or they can be externally generated (e.g. job insecurity, an unstable marriage etc.) Mostly your stress-picture will be an amalgam of internally and externally originating factors. Attitudes, beliefs, behaviour patterns, personality traits (the major features of the hardiness factor: control, challenge and commitment) and deeply entrenched habits of thought may all be partly responsible, and I shall explain several ways of examining and modifying them. The importance of correct nutrition, sufficient exercise and rest, as well as such things as adequate exposure to full spectrum light (daylight), will be other themes which I touch on in as much as they relate to stress reduction and to our aim of stress-proofing ourselves.

These areas are important, but the main point of this book is to show that there are defences which can be erected against stress, whatever form it takes, and that by the regular application of these methods great benefit can be derived in terms of health and well-being. We must certainly aim at reducing stress, but must also increase our resistance to it and learn to counteract its effects.

Effective stress-proofing, therefore, involves taking responsibility; which means incorporating positive action in various areas of your life. For, it is necessary and desirable to understand not just the causes of stress, but also the physiological and pathological effects which it can produce, and the ways in which its negative tendencies can be countered. For the very best results such strategies need to be combined with methods which effectively increase and enhance the natural defences against stress, which some people have in greater or lesser degree than others. The importance of reviewing, and altering where necessary, your diet, exercise and rest patterns, lifestyle and personal attitude, as well as behaviour patterns (many of which are within our conscious control) are all features of this comprehensive protection plan which can deflect many of the potentially harmful effects of hectic modern-day life.

Next, I present a number of different breathing exercises and patterns, and relaxation methods, as well as a selection of meditation techniques, together with a résumé of current thinking on the use of mind/body therapies, such as visualization, which emphasize the power of the mind in promoting good health.

One of the quickest ways in which your blood chemistry can be disturbed under stress conditions, producing a host of symptoms – ranging from feelings of intense agitation and weakness to anxiety and panic attacks, as well as physical effects such as numbness of the limbs, nausea, stomach cramps and shivering – is by hyperventilation. In Chapter 6 I give a detailed explanation of this widespread phenomenon of over-breathing, and show how it can usually be dealt with swiftly by using special breathing techniques which almost anyone can learn to apply to themselves.

Whilst the process by which hyperventilation affects us is relatively easy to grasp, there are other aspects of stress's interaction with our minds and nervous systems which are quite complex. One is the effect of the state of mind on the immune (defence) system of our bodies. The new science which concerns itself with this side of things is called *psychoneuroimmunology*, and it deserves to be more widely understood, for it holds the key to many common and some serious health problems.

The discovery and proof of the existence of this mind/immune system link was made as far back as 1975 by Dr Robert Ader, a psychologist at the University of Rochester in the USA. He had been studying the effects of giving laboratory rats an unpleasant drug-induced sensation of nausea every time they drank water which had been sweetened with saccharine. He was in fact studying the phenomenon of conditioned response, made famous (some would say notorious) by Pavlov in his dog experiments half a century previously. Just as Pavlov's dogs learned to salivate whenever a bell was rung (through having been conditioned by a bell being rung whenever they were fed), so did Ader's rats learn to feel sick whenever they were allowed to drink sweet water.

In itself this result was not sufficient to attract attention, but what Ader observed next was of profound importance. He saw that not only did his rats dutifully become sick whenever they had sweetened water (even after the drug injections had ceased), they soon began to really sicken and to die. The reason, he found, was that the drug he had been using to induce a feeling of sickness was an immune depressing substance. So, not only had the rats learned to feel sick when they drank the sweet water, they also mimicked the other immune suppressing effects of the drug, even long after the drug administration had ceased, producing in themselves a reduction of immune function. As a result they went on to die of auto-immune diseases or overwhelming infection allowed to occur through their self-induced immune response suppression.

This was surely proof positive that the mind can control immune function directly, and that it could switch off the defence mechanism sufficiently to allow serious illness and death to occur. Much additional evidence has subsequently been produced which supports Ader's original observations. Does this also apply to humans? Indeed it does, and many medical studies have proved it to the extent that researchers are being led to the conclusion that it is not stress which does the damage, but how we handle it. This is something we should be sure to take heed of.

A leading article in the 27 June 1987 edition of the *Lancet*, one of Britain's most prestigious medical journals, under the title of 'Depression, stress and immunity', came to the conclusion that 'it is the individual's response to stress that determines the effects on immunity rather than the stress itself.' This statement is of profound importance and deserves illustration.

One easy measurement of immune function can be made by studying the efficiency, or otherwise, of a group of defensive cells which go by the name of 'natural killer cells'. Their function is termed 'natural killer cell activity' (NKCA). When this was measured in groups of medical students before an important examination, NKCA was found to be depressed in some but not in others. These observations were then compared with psychological profiles previously conducted on the same students, and it was discovered that they related directly; that is, those students who were known to be 'poor copers' (high levels of reported life stress accompanied by health distress), or subject to loneliness (social isolation) were also the students with poor NKCA at exam time. In contrast, those who were good copers (high life stress but little health distress) had continued high performance in the NKCA when confronted by examination stresses.

It is no surprise that the poor copers were the ones who became ill with colds, 'flu etc., since their immune function was inadequate when faced by infectious agents. The stress of exams was the same for all the students, and this presents a clear picture of where the cause lies – not with stress alone, but with the way it was handled. Numerous studies confirm this. As the famous American surgeon, Bernie Siegel, MD, states: 'The medical profession is going to have to confront this thing we call the mind.'

Research at the National Institute for Mental Health in America by Candace Pert, a neuropharmacologist, has shown that substances called neuropeptides, which are messenger molecules which interact between the nervous system and the immune system (in all animal and plant life) appear to unify the multiple interacting systems in the body so that they act in concert to survive, unless negative health-destroying factors are at work. This may well be the way psychological factors interact with the immune system. This new knowledge is summarized quite graphically by the words of another American researcher, Robert Cathcart, MD, who says: 'All the vitamin C in the world won't make up for a lousy attitude.'

Among the chemical changes found to take place in the brain in response to stress, sometimes within seconds, are increased production of neurotransmitters such as serotonin, epinephrin (what used to be called adrenalin), acetylcholine and dopamine, all of which increase the excitability of nerve cells.

It is therefore abundantly clear where we need to focus our attention if we are to avoid those aspects of ill-health which relate to stress. As the *Lancet* puts it: 'The efforts of psychologists, counsellors and indeed general practitioners may be of more value . . . were they to concentrate on improving coping skills and increasing people's sense of self-efficacy . . . for fortunately all these procedures [learning of coping skills] can be taught.' So, according to the most respected medical opinion, we can learn to handle stress and many of its negative influences on the body chemistry and immune function.

A variety of techniques exist in this field, some more suited to a particular person than others. The main aim of this book is to enable the reader to find those methods that best suit him or her, and to explain how important their regular use is in regaining and maintaining health. Whether active or passive relaxation methods are employed, or whether meditation alone, or together with creative visualization and guided imagery, is found to produce the desired results, is immaterial.

What matters is that we learn to harness the mind's latent force towards positive rather than negative goals, and that the mind/body complex is insulated, as far as possible, from those internally and externally generated stresses which, left unchecked, will first weaken, then cripple and finally destroy the body.

Health and disease, and all the grey area between, are states which reflect the ability, or otherwise, of the body to maintain equilibrium (known as homoeostasis) in the face of a host of environmental threats and hazards. At any given time the individual represents a culmination of all that has been inherited, and all that has been acquired and developed up to that moment. The degrees of susceptibility and of resistance that the body can demonstrate, will be absolutely unique to him or her. With so many variables, it should be obvious that no one method, system or prescription can apply to everyone, even if similar outward manifestations of ill health are evident.

Because of this, less emphasis should perhaps be placed on outward signs and symptoms of ill health. Whilst these are important, they indicate no more than how the individual is responding to a health threat. The same symptoms (e.g. headache) can result from a variety of causes. The same apparent cause (e.g. anxiety) can produce quite different symptoms – say insomnia in one person, palpitations in another and headaches in a third.

Treatment of the symptoms alone can never bring more than short-term relief. To remove the symptoms and ignore the cause is patently wrong, for they or other symptoms will surely re-show themselves sooner or later. Only by improving the general level of function of the total organism and by removing, where possible, the causes of the condition, can a successful outcome be anticipated.

Since causes of anxiety are often outside the control of the individual, it is necessary to provide ways of altering the ways in which such problems are viewed. In addition, techniques are necessary whereby, even if such stress remains to some extent constant, the individual can nullify and counteract its ill effects by positive action. This is where relaxation, meditation and other exercises of the mind come in.

Additional methods, which will be explained in Chapter 8, are derived from the work of a remarkable researcher, L.E. Eeman. The approaches which he evolved include application of the knowledge that we all have what appear to be specific 'polarities' in different parts of the body, and that it is possible to use this fact in a practical way in order to enable deep relaxation to be achieved.

Using electromagnetic terminology, Eeman proved that 'when different parts of one human body, or different or similar parts of different human bodies are connected by means of electrical conductors, such as insulated copper wires, these bodies behave as though (using an electromagnetic analogy) they were bi-polar.' The polar opposites which Eeman identified most strongly were the head and base of the spine, and the right and left hands. The effect achieved by holding a piece of insulated copper wire in one hand, attached to a copper grid lying under the spine or head (with no connection whatever to external electrical supply) is to produce either an increase in relaxation or tension, depending upon whether the hand and the part of the body involved had similar or opposite polarities.

For example, should the right hand (of a born right-handed person) be linked with the base of the spine (these being polar opposites) the result is a 'relaxation circuit', while connection of the right hand with the base of the head (here the polarities are the same) causes a 'tension circuit'. 'The relaxation circuit automatically promotes relaxation of the voluntary muscles and stimulates functional activity. It fosters sleep, recovery from fatigue and disease, capacity for work and health in general. The tension circuit reverses these effects, more or less. Both circuits affect not only organic, but also nervous and mental health.'

In Chapter 8 a number of useful methods, based on Eeman's work, are described, including two self-help approaches, one of which calls for the use of copper wire and gauze, and another which does not.

Stress-proofing is all about choices. No one pattern of relaxation exercise can possibly suit everyone, and this is the reason for the presence in this book of a wide variety of options. Try the ones that appeal to you. Drop those that do not work easily, and hold fast to those that do. There is certainly no sense in trying methods which just do not appeal or those that you feel uneasy with. Remember, though, that there is a rule of thumb which, stated simply, insists that until you know how to breathe adequately relaxation is difficult, if not impossible, and that it is virtually impossible to use the methods of guided imagery and visualization until you can meditate.

This means that whichever choices you eventually make in terms of which methods, or patterns, of relaxation, meditation and visualization you use, there is need for that sequence   (breathing-relaxation-meditation-visualization) to be respected, if good results are to be hoped for.

The individuality of each person must be recognized; this leads to a realization that the particular factors which enable successful adaptation to the environment will vary. Stress-proofing involves gaining understanding and insight into the nature of the problems of stress, as well as a determination to make changes, alterations, modifications and efforts in accordance with this knowledge. Through this apparent maze, I would urge you to hold fast to one concrete thought: given the chance, the body is a self-healing, self-repairing and self-regenerating organism. The aim is to give it that chance, and at the same time to erect barriers which will provide protection against future hazards.

CHAPTER 1

The Causes and Nature of Stress

Stress-induced illnesses now cause more deaths and diseases than do infections, which used to be the predominant killer in industrialized countries. Among those conditions now known, in many instances, to involve the interaction of stress and particular personality 'types' are arthritis, cardiovascular disease, respiratory disease, cancer and depression. It has also been shown beyond doubt that 'noxious' factors, such as negative emotion, anxiety, grief, loneliness and depression are actually immune suppressive, contributing in large part to subsequent illness and often death.

Excitingly, and of major importance in our quest for better health, research has also revealed that whatever it takes to create a 'distress-free' mind produces as a consequence beneficial immune-enhancing effects. Indeed, just as Ader was able to show that he could condition rats to become immune compromised, so can improved immunity be conditioned (R. Gorcynski, 'Conditioned immune response associated with allogenic skin grafts', *Journal of Immunology* (1982), Vol. 220, pages 821-2). Animals and humans can 'learn' to become healthier and to have improved immune activity.

It is of only partial value to concentrate on just one side

of the picture, to think only of stress avoidance or of better stress handling. Ideally, both elements of the stress/health equation should be looked at and, if possible, dealt with. You need to be aware that stress is at its most harmful when you respond to it inappropriately.

Most stress situations in today's life are not as simple as the 'fight or flight' reaction, when the stress is matched by a straightforward immediately executed response. There may be no obvious choices to make, and in many instances there is no on-the-spot 'caveman' solution – for example, when you are exposed to someone's rudeness or aggressive behaviour, and you metaphorically have to 'take it on the chin'. Repeated exercising of pretended patience may indeed result in stress-induced damage. Many stressful events in life, such as divorce, bereavement, loss of a job, etc., present no opportunity for a simple and immediate 'fight or flight' response, and how they affect us depends very much on our emotional coping skills.

Equally damaging are reactions which are inappropriate. For example, when anger is the response to an incident which someone else would treat as being of little importance – in other words, an over-reaction. The question is: how is it that some people can cope with all these things, whilst others cannot? The answer is a matter of attitude, belief and habitual behavioural patterns.

Many of our attitudes derive from the imprinting we receive in our early formative years. Unconsciously we are 'programmed' by what we hear and see as children, and these attitudes then become the blueprints, the beliefs, which dictate how we will 'feel', act and respond in a multitude of situations, including stressful ones.

It is our acceptance when very young, usually without question or critical judgement, of the attitudes we see and learn from our parents, relatives, friends, schools etc. which mould our later behaviour and responses to stress. To alter entrenched attitudes and behaviour in later life we first must recognize that we may be 'programmed' in a manner which leads to inappropriate, self-damaging behaviour, and that just as we first learned attitudes when we were very young, so can we re-learn a different view of life later if we wish to.

The key to such a change is awareness of where the key to improving things lies, to a realization that there are other ways of seeing things, that these may be more life/health enhancing than our current approaches, that we need to challenge our present attitudes and beliefs. As you alter your attitudes so will your feelings change, and this is because it is your thoughts which govern your emotions. If you can learn to see your emotions as a mirror of your thoughts, and if you are aware that your emotions are in turmoil, or that they lead you to inappropriate responses, you can see that it is the way you think which needs to be addressed before changes will come in your emotions and stress-coping skills.

If you can begin to see that a repetitive cycle occurs in which life stresses are poorly coped with, and that the end result of this is depression, and the risk of mental and physical ill health, the need to gain control of the underlying causes becomes clear. Control of the emotions comes through understanding and awareness that negative feelings can be replaced with positive ones.

It is no simple or easy task to make such changes, and it may well require professional counselling, for it is not enough to simply superficially 'blot out' negative emotions with an overlay of positive thinking. What is called for is a more fundamental change in which you come to understand your way of thinking, the place where your attitudes were born. The start of this process towards an upwards positive spiral is recognition of what is necessary, followed by the use of a method which leads to greater understanding or insight. This can be achieved by attending workshops or group therapy sessions, or one-to-one counselling with a therapist, whether the method involves psychosynthesis, voice dialogue, neurolinguistic programming, or any other humanistic psychotherapy tool.

In all of these methods, judgements are avoided, and understanding and awareness is encouraged. Once you come to understand and accept yourself, and learn why you think (and, therefore, behave) as you do, change comes naturally.

There are a number of defensive tricks which the mind can play in response to any challenge or stress. These include repression of thoughts and memories which might prove stressful, as well as 'rationalization', in which the individual makes up an account of his or her behaviour in response to stress, the true explanation of which would produce anxiety. Such common defences, if producing anxiety states or personality changes, require professional psychotherapy to provide insights into, and resolution of, the problem.

It is self-evident, then, that what is to one individual a major stress factor may to another be only a minor irritant. Recall the student doctors who I referred to earlier. Some became ill and some did not when confronted by the same exam stresses. It was their coping skills and attitudes which determined who would become ill and who would not. In a well-documented study (M. Linn, 'Stressful events, disphoric mood and immune responsiveness', *Psychological Report* (1984), Vol. 54, pages 219-22) it was shown that the psychological response to a stressful event can alter the ability of the immune system to function adequately. In particular, men who reported the most depression after bereavement or serious family illness had the greatest reduction in immune efficiency. Such changes are not confined to depressive illness, but may result in a variety of responses to unpleasant life events.

Now, it is clear that life-events are common to us all. We all experience many, or even most, of the sort of events which are listed below, and yet they do not provoke a negative effect in everyone. Dr Norman Cousins, writing in the *American Journal of Holistic Medicine* (March/April 1986, pages 1-20) gives his view of the remedy which saves so many from stress-induced illness.

'If negative emotions like panic can create disease, what is the role of positive emotions – love, hope, faith, laughter, playfulness, creativity? I've come to the conclusion that the function of the positive emotions is to interrupt the negative ones. The positive emotions protect the body against the bolts of fear, anger, worry and despair. They are the blockers, magnificent blockers . . . blocking as they can the disease of panic, which can intensify virtually any underlying illness. It is not possible to entertain two contrary feelings. The positive emotions drive out the negative. You cannot panic and laugh at the same time.'

The difference lies in a person's attitude towards the cause of stress. For one person, for example, the meeting of a deadline, the need to be at a particular place at a fixed time, is of vital importance, and the prospect of being late, of failing to meet the deadline, generates a great deal of tension and anxiety. To another person, such deadlines are mere guidelines, and no particular worry is felt at their being missed.

Attitudes depend upon a person's concept of reality. The world as they see it is their own reality, and when this comes into conflict with the external environment stress results. To some extent, all change represents stress. Anything that calls on us to adjust or change from what is normal represents stress. Our concept of what is normal, what is right, how things ought to be is, therefore, the sounding board on which the external environmental factors operate. Beliefs and attitudes often determine the degree of stress, anxiety etc. experienced. For example, the death of someone close is undoubtedly a major stress factor, and yet to someone whose beliefs include a certainty of an after-life or a reincarnation, the death will be seen as part of a continuous process, not an end, and therefore the amount of stress will be minimized. Clearly, what you believe, what you think, and how you see both major and minor events, is linked to your learned responses, which in turn derives from your upbringing and the attitudes and beliefs of those who guided your early years, modified by all that has happened to you since then.

Stress and Changes in Lifestyle

It has been possible to grade the potential of events or changes in our life. In the following chart, scores have been allotted to each event so that the degree of susceptibility to the effects of stress can be estimated. This can be valuable in alerting us to pay extra attention to dealing with those elements of health maintenance which are within our control. Some such methods are explained in Chapter 5.

The stress scale is based on the work of T.H. Holmes and R.H. Rahe (*Journal of Psychosomatic Research* (1967), No. 11) and is meant as a guide to the assessment of measurable stress resulting from having to adjust to change. There are many other causes of stress, but it is true to say that a high score on this chart (300 or more) over a short period of time (six months or so) is a strong indicator (affecting 80 per cent of us) that a major illness may follow. If the score is relatively high (anything from 150 to 299) about 50 per cent of us may become ill soon afterwards, and if under 150 points are scored, fewer than 30 per cent become ill. The higher the score the greater the need for stress-proofing.

Changes in lifestyle	Scale
Death of spouse	100
Divorce	73
Marital separation	65
Jail sentence or being institutionalized	63
Death of close member of family	63
Illness or injury	53
Marriage	50

Changes in lifestyle	*Scale*
Loss of job	47
Reconciliation with marriage partner	45
Retirement	45
Health problem of close member of family	44
Pregnancy	40
Sex problems	39
Addition to family	39
Major change at work	39
Change of financial status	39
Death of a friend	37
Change in line of work	36
Change in number of marital arguments	35
Large mortgage taken out	31
Mortgage or loan foreclosed	30
Responsibility change	29
Child leaves home	29
In-law problems	29
Personal achievement realized	28
Wife starts or stops work	26
Starting a new school	26
Leaving school	26
Change in living conditions	25
Change in personal habits	24
Trouble with employer	23
Change in working hours	20
Change in residence	20
Change in recreation	19
Change in church activities	19
Change in social activities	18
Small mortgage taken out	17
Change in sleeping habits	16
Change in number of family get-togethers	15
Major change in eating pattern	15
Holiday	13
Christmas	12
Minor violation of the law	11

It is known that these scores and the position on the scale of some of the incidents vary in different cultures. Different belief systems place the stress of marriage higher in Europe, for example, than in Japan. It can also be seen from the list that stress factors are not always confined to unpleasant events. A holiday, for instance, is seen as a cause of stress. Change itself, pleasant or unpleasant, has a potential for stress. But, even in high-scoring people 20 per cent do not become ill soon afterwards because it is our response, our attitudes, beliefs and underlying health status, that are the real determining factors in whether or not we are badly affected by stress. The list can be used as a guide, but it should be coupled with thoughts on the most appropriate responses, and these responses should then be cultivated.

Anticipated problems

There is another element in life which can often produce even more stress than events and changes which actually take place. This is the highly charged area of anticipated problems or events. Whilst losing a job is indeed a high-scoring stress factor, the anticipation of such a loss presents potentially greater stresses by virtue of the time-scale involved. Once a job has been lost, the reality of the situation determines that the person concerned does something about it. Looking for a new job, making practical arrangements regarding finance etc. are all stressful, but they are positive responses to the event. If, however, there are rumours of possible redundancies, and the anxiety and uncertainty continues for months or years, then the stress induced may be far greater. It is, nevertheless, worth remembering that, in such a case, there are practical steps which can be taken to minimize the effects of the stress once it is realized what is happening.

So, apart from actual changes in life being potentially

stressful, the anticipation of such changes also creates stress. It is true, too, unfortunately, that much stress relates to an inability to resolve events which are in the past. Guilt, self-pity, brooding over events gone by – real or imagined – present another major potential for stress generation. Not only does such dwelling on the past produce stressful changes in the body, but it greatly diminishes our ability to function well in the present.

As well as anticipated or remembered unpleasant events, stress can build up from the environment in which we find ourselves. We may have to work amongst a lot of noise, or in very hot or cold conditions. All these things, including the effects of change, are termed 'stressors', and of course their potential for harm will depend upon our attitudes, emotions and personality characteristics. The strain, conflict and pressure resulting from such stressors may produce anxiety states which can be short-lived or long-term. Since it is not possible, in the main, to protect oneself against the major changes in life, it should be thought of as desirable and necessary that attitudes should be cultivated which will minimize the effects of the inevitable vicissitudes of life.

External stressors, whilst easy to identify, are less easy to measure and control. These might include difficult working conditions, boring repetitive occupations, and commuting on an unreliable transport system, or having to drive in heavy traffic for hours every day. Our bodies respond to all such stressors in a predictable pattern of internal changes. Stress is, however, cumulative, and a relatively minor event, when added to a large existing stress load, will often prove to be more than the body's adaptation process can cope with. To a large extent the breaking point can be avoided by taking care of that aspect of the stress jigsaw puzzle most easily alterable, i.e. your personal habits and lifestyle. A change in attitude can dramatically alter the potential for damage created by externally generated stress, but such a change is far more difficult to achieve than, for example, a healthier pattern of rest and exercise, or a change in the food you eat.

Challenge and Control: The Element of Choice

All the changes and challenges in your life require that you adapt to or deal with them, often on a level where you are acting instinctively. Such challenges of life might involve any of the seemingly mundane stressors referred to above, or such things as:

- Time pressures (deadlines, appointments, responsibilities, tasks, tests, meetings)
- Other people's behaviour (abusive, unkind, unreliable, contradictory, demanding, spiteful)
- Situations (job or home pressures, expectations of others)
- Self-imposed stresses (excessively high standards of performance in job, and even leisure activity; unduly self-critical)
- Life events beyond your control (as listed on pages 24 and 25) or the prospect of these

The question of whether or not damaging stress will result from any of these or other challenges and demands hinges upon the type of response which is forthcoming. Are the challenges seen as something to be overcome, to be dealt with, to grow through, offering a spur towards an improved future, triggers for potential growth, opportunity for change for the better? Or are they viewed as insurmountable, never-ending, overwhelming, crushing, beyond any personal control, negative with no redeeming features at all? To a large extent the degree of stress-induced damage which occurs is dependent upon which answer is forthcoming to these questions.

It is the 'hardy' response which is health-promoting with quite the opposite effect deriving from the opposite choice. Hardiness carries with it a sense of being in control, the view that the sort of events and situations described above offer a challenge and not a threat, and finally a sense of involvement and commitment rather than of detachment and isolation. And, in all of these hardiness elements, whether or not you feel it likely at this stage, you have a large degree of choice.

Choice? Yes indeed, for we can learn to choose how we will respond to life's inconsistencies, demands and challenges, and this represents a major element in stress-proofing yourself. Even your believing the possibility of that statement being correct involves choice.

From childhood onwards, stress provides a spur and an incentive to development. The will to please others and to satisfy inner drives are responses to needs, desires and targets or goals, set by authority, society, family, self, and so on. This aspect of stress is vital to human survival and development. It is when there are inappropriate responses to such drives that stress becomes potentially harmful.

Whether considering early childhood development, schooling, family life, courtship, marriage, higher education, work or retirement, life presents a kaleidoscope of stressful events, challenges, obstacles, pitfalls and sometimes tragedies. The ground on which these events fall is the personality and make-up of the person, and since the avoidance of all stressful events and stages in life is not possible, it is the ground, the personality and belief system, that presents the main opportunity for modification, and consequent lessening of the impact of the many stressors that beset us.

'Type A' and 'Type B' Personalities

Cardiologists, Friedman and Rosenmann, have described the 'Type A' personality who is predisposed to heart disease. The Type A individual moves, walks, talks and eats quickly. He finds it difficult to relax, sets himself deadlines, often undertakes more than one task at a time; he fidgets and is ambitious. The 'Type B' person, much less prone to heart disease, is in direct contrast. This type moves, talks and eats slowly, is able to relax, is unambitious and avoids pressure and deadlines. None of this is too surprising, but what is exciting is that, when motivated (often by an early coronary) the Type A can turn into a Type B by altering their behaviour and copying Type B behaviour until it becomes habitual. There is a consequent drop in the likelihood of coronary disease following such a modification. Type A will have then adopted more desirable and appropriate responses to the needs of life, and will have enhanced his chances of long-term survival.

Living in the present lessens the tendency to dwell on past events or to worry about anticipated future events, and a further aspect of this is that the nearer our concept of reality is to actual life the less stress will be created. Reality may not always be the same for all people, but in many daily situations the stress felt by people is the direct result of their 'fantasy' of how things should be, being at odds with reality. *My* 'fantasy', for example, is that when people make appointments they ought to keep them, and what is more, they ought to be on time. In reality, however, this is often not the case. The annoyance and stress which is generated every time an appointment is missed or someone is late, could be avoided if I could bring my fantasy closer to real life, i.e. anticipate that people will, by the nature of things, be late for or will actually forget to keep their appointments from time to time.

'If Only . . .'

In terms of attitudes to life and events, such thoughts or utterances as 'if only . . .' or 'it should have been like . . .', or 'wouldn't it have been nice if . . .' indicate a failure to accept reality, or an unwillingness to accept what has actually happened. This type of 'fantasy' may appear harmless, but it is as potentially stressful as dwelling in the past or future. It is, in fact, another facet of that same tendency. 'Be there now' is the best piece of advice for such a person to bear in mind. Life is in the 'here and now'. In the past, the future and the 'if only' lie shadows, demons and stress.

Nowhere is this more evident than in personal relationships, whether this be at work or in the home environment. Much stress results from an inability to express feelings clearly, without becoming upset. If feelings are expressed inadequately, then hostility and anger will often develop. Once again, many such stresses relate to differences of opinion as to what is, and what is not reality. Interpersonal relationships require that we express our feelings clearly and in a non-hostile manner, and that we are then prepared to listen to a similar expression of the other person's views, without feeling 'got at' or under attack.

This is the ideal, of course, and it may be difficult to achieve because of long-held attitudes and firmly-rooted personality traits, but it is, undoubtedly, the way to ensure non-stressful relationships. Seeing reality in the present, the ability to deliver unbiased, non-hostile expressions of opinion, and the ability to listen are, then, qualities to be cultivated.

In personal relationships much tension is generated as a result of unfulfilled expectations. If one party anticipates a gesture or form of recognition (such as a birthday card or telephone call) which does not materialize, a tense and resentful attitude may ensue. Again, an ability to communicate can defuse such a situation. Errors or sins of omission are just as potentially stressful as sins of commission; i.e. non-events as opposed to actual events. If bottled up and nursed, such feelings can produce stress out of all proportion to the importance of the actual incident.

Self-Esteem and Cynicism

Into the huge equation of stress factors and their interaction with the mind/body complex which makes up each of us, we need to add 'self-image'. How do you see yourself in relation to others, society at large, your friends and family? How accurately (and how harshly) do you judge your own strengths and weaknesses? Above all, what is the degree of your self-esteem, and how important is that anyway?

An important leading article appeared in the *Lancet* (22 October 1988, pages 943-4) which addressed the question of self-esteem. This explained the complex way in which we come to a value judgement, in which we weigh ourselves, deriving our standards partly by comparing ourselves with others. Do we, however, compare ourselves with those who are better off or those who are worse off than ourselves?

Modern American adolescents compare themselves with their fellows, judging by such yardsticks as popularity, degree of influence over others, school and other results and their self-awareness of such concepts as honour and virtue. Out of those assessments comes a self-esteem judgement which can profoundly influence the person's stress-coping abilities.

In adult life we use similar yardsticks, but we add to it factors such as how good we feel we have been at being parents, husbands or wives, as well as experiences of success and failure in many of life's tasks and the world in general. One common tactic in maintaining self-esteem is the awarding to ourselves of the credit for all that goes well, and to others (or circumstances) the blame for all that goes wrong.

Additional reinforcement for feelings of self-esteem (and the opposite) derives from other people's opinions of us, as we perceive them. To that we have to add the degree of respect, attention, approval, praise, affection and love (or the opposite of any of these) we receive. Our self-esteem, therefore, has a lot to do with how we see our value reflected in the eyes of those around us and of society, and this starts in childhood.

Freud summed it up by saying: 'A man who has been the indisputable favourite of his mother keeps for life the feeling of a conqueror.' Imagine also the opposite, the sense of rejection and failure which children derive and carry with them into adult life from a parental attitude of indifference, or worse. Of course, life is seldom as simple as any of these models suggest. Some children are much loved by their parents, but rejected by their peers (or the other way around); some people regard themselves as superior, having a high self-esteem, despite little evidence that anyone else agrees with them.

Is Self-Esteem Important Anyway?

It is known that poor self-esteem is linked to illness such as depression, anxiety states and a host of psychosomatic disorders. It has also been linked to delinquency, child abuse and prejudice. It is even suggested, with strong research evidence, that our measuring of self-esteem has echoes in biological evolution. Many animals have displayed what is called 'resource holding potential' (RHP). This relates to the animal's sense of degree of ability to fight and defend itself when it compares itself with other animals. When a low RHP is assessed by an animal it actually alters its internal physiological state, characterized by excretion of higher levels of certain hormones, changes in skin colour and behaviour patterns which indicate submission rather than a desire to assert itself. This sort of behaviour is clear to anyone who has kept groups of animals in which some dominate and others seem willing to adopt submissive roles (the pecking order in a chicken run is a good example.)

In a human setting this means that hardiness, self-esteem, the ability to deal with life's vicissitudes, could be linked to the primeval pattern noted in our animal example, and that we unconsciously take on the role of the weak and vulnerable based largely on our self-image, our degree or lack of self-esteem, and that this has profound implications in health terms. Unlike chickens, we are not legally permitted to assert ourselves by pecking and fighting, and we should look for other ways of raising self-esteem. This has to be one of the major challenges of stress-proofing. And, what is the ideal? To be healthy, it is suggested, you should be neither unmoved by success nor indifferent to it. You should also be using every means possible to increase awareness in yourself of these self-imposed limitations, so that you can blossom into the full potential which life offers, even with all its challenges and hardships.

But can self-esteem itself lead to excesses?

Cynicism

A danger inherent in excessively high self-esteem is seen in behaviour involving cynical mistrust. This is character-ized by a collection of attitudes which involves suspicion and the denigration of the motives and behaviour of others, and this has been shown to be a risk factor in the development of coronary heart disease (A. Fontana et al , 'Cynical mistrust and the search for self-worth', *Journal of Psychosomatic Research* (1989), Vol. 33, No. 4, pages 449-56.)

Interestingly, this research also showed that such people who are prone to self-criticism if they fail to reach the high standards they set themselves, who score high in assessment of their own self-worth in social comparisons as well as displaying cynical mistrust of others, also scored high in assessment of their degree of dependency on others for validation that they were deserving of being loved.

Self-esteem can therefore be seen to be a two-edged sword, especially where these other elements are found (cynical mistrust and strongly self-critical tendencies). I will return to cynicism in later chapters, and will also examine a splendid psychotherapeutic tool (Voice Dialogue) which allows the therapist to help you become aware of the 'sub-personalities' which make up all of us, and which can be involved in these excesses of critical and self-critical behaviour.

In summary: self-esteem, in its healthiest expressions, is a major stress-proofing factor, and conversely excessive self-esteem, especially when linked with cynicism, is a stress factor in its own right, as is low self-esteem.

Basic Emotions

The range of possible stress factors is almost endless, and the possible permutations of reaction to them equally so. It has been said that there are only two basic emotions: 'like' and 'dislike'. All other emotions stem from variations and degrees of these prime feelings. The amazing differences in people, tastes, likes, dislikes and so on, makes it obvious that there is seldom any intrinsic quality in an event, object or situation, which guarantees it being universally liked or disliked (one man's meat is patently another man's poison). It is also worth noting that at different stages in life and under different conditions, the same person's 'likes' and 'dislikes' will vary.

The conclusion may be drawn that a person can possibly be taught to like what was previously disliked, and vice versa. Thus, if, because of degrees of 'liking' or 'disliking', a person's behaviour gives rise to a more stressful existence and more problematic relationships than are desirable, reduction of stress is possible only through a basic change in attitudes.

Just as type A must change from a fast-moving, fast-talking, fast-acting, fast-eating individual to one with more deliberate habits, so must the individual who says 'that's how I am, I can't change!' be made to understand that change is not only possible but desirable, and that self-interest dictates that it should be so. Changing habits and attitudes is merely a matter of understanding and recognizing them for what they are, followed by modifications in behaviour. This is easily said and, obviously, not as easily achieved. However, as will become clear, the alternatives to such behavioural modification may often be serious illness.

The Importance of Changing Your Automatic Response

In setting about behavioural modification – the changing of habitual attitudes and ways of responding – it is important to be aware that whenever you behave in a particular manner, you reinforce the belief that lies behind that form of behaviour. If there is always an angry tantrum in response to real or imagined criticism, then your belief that this is the appropriate response will be reinforced with each outburst.

To alter the underlying belief calls for an altered response. By substituting a less stressful, less provocative reaction, the belief will develop, and be reinforced, that the new reaction is correct and appropriate. Obviously, in interpersonal relationships, two such modified responses may be needed, and this is not easy to arrange.

Once you realize the role that habit plays in reinforcing undesirable modes of behaviour, it is possible to begin to change. By acting in a manner in which the other person is dealt with as you would wish to be dealt with yourself, and by expressing whatever needs to be said honestly and calmly, the opportunity will grow for a less stressful relationship. Such behaviour changes often spark changes for the better in the other half of the relationship.

It is worth noting that no-one and nothing makes you angry. You do it all on your own. Such feelings are always self-generated, and this is true of most emotions. You choose to be angry, jealous, guilty or bitter and, equally, you choose to be happy, giving, loving etc. Your attitudes and behaviour can be self-modified, and most experiences present a choice of response – one negative and stressful, and the other positive and, potentially, offering the opportunity for growth and self-knowledge – that choice always being yours, and the extent of attention you pay to the stress-reducing measures presented later in this book will be an indication of the extent to which you are prepared to accept responsibility for your life and actions.

Stress is Cumulative

Whilst, in early life, most people can cope with a great deal of emotional and physical trauma, this ability tends to diminish as life progresses. There are, of course, inherited characteristics which have an influence on our capacity for coping. And, there are other factors which will also, to varying degrees, determine to what extent stress can influence our physical and mental health. Among these are nutritional considerations, structural factors, exercise patterns, general fatigue, and the sum total – long-term and in the recent past – of stress. The effects these influences have will become clearer in subsequent chapters. At this stage, it is worth noting that stress is the spur that moves us to action, and that, if responses are not appropriate, it can also become the boulder that crushes.

There is indeed a point at which our body's capacity for adjustment and adaptation in the face of stress becomes inadequate. When this occurs, health begins to break down in obvious ways. I will cover this in greater detail in the next chapter, but it is important to note that this very noticeable deterioration in health is itself a potent stressor. Anxiety in the face of changes in function and the onset of pain quickens the downward spiral. If you wait for this stage before taking reforming action you may have waited too long. It is, though, possible to regain health from this point, but only with great effort.

There are extrinsic factors which are outside our control, but there are also many aspects of the picture that we can control. There are, of course, states of mind which generate stress, which are outside our conscious control. There are many deep-seated anxiety states and depressions, in which only skilled psychotherapy and counselling can enable us to achieve insights and understanding and, ultimately, a resolution of the problem. Such forms of treatment lie outside the scope of this book, but it is suggested that the general principles here outlined, and the techniques described, can only be of help, even in such cases. However, no-one who is receiving psychotherapy should attempt self-treatment without first consulting his or her practitioner.

CHAPTER 2

The Physical Effects of Stress

Stress is an essential and constant part of life. It is the spur that drives humankind to all achievement, but, when excessive, it can destroy. All the ages and stages of life are transitional; from baby to toddler, from schoolchild to young adult, from active worker to retired pensioner, and so on. Each change has potential stress implications which, when overlayed upon the external and internal stresses of living, are constantly affecting our minds and bodies.

A definition of stress, coined by the great researcher into this ubiquitous phenomenon, Dr Hans Selye, is simply 'the rate of wear and tear on the body'. All change calls for adaptation. If we go from a warm room into the freezing cold outdoors, adaptive mechanisms immediately become operative to help the body to maintain its equilibrium.

Adaptive processes take place in response to all changes and stressors, whether these are physical, such as heat and cold; chemical, such as polluted air and water, and drugs; or self-generated emotions, such as anger, grief or joy. Anything that is perceived as threatening the mind or body arouses a response of an adaptive or defensive nature instantly.

Homoeostasis

This ability to attempt to maintain the safe equilibrium of the body is known as homoeostasis. It is, for a variety of reasons, not always successful. The biochemistry of the body may be inadequate for the task, perhaps through poor nutrition – and this and other possible factors, including structural integrity, will be considered later. If the response is inadequate, or if perception of threats is inaccurate, then unbalanced and faulty body adjustments may occur with harmful consequences.

The normal stress reaction is seldom the result of the outside agency, but rather it is the system's reaction to it. Whether the stressor is physical, such as sudden exposure to cold; or psychological, such as an unexpected crisis or a change of responsibility at work, or unpleasant news, the body begins to make biochemical changes in response to its perceived needs. Such changes take place to a greater or lesser degree almost constantly throughout life.

If a stressor is prolonged, continuous or extreme in its nature, then the defensive mechanisms of the body become even more active. In response to intense heat, changes take place in the blood chemistry and circulatory system in order to cool the body by means, for example, of extra fluid loss and evaporation through the skin. Should this fail to achieve the desired effect, then an even greater defensive effort might involve fainting and temporary unconsciousness, in order to reduce all bodily functions to a minimum. Such homoeostatic efforts, though, fall short of being actual stress reactions, unless prolonged.

Fight or Flight

In response to any stress or extreme the body undergoes a series of changes which Selye has grouped under the heading of the 'fight or flight' reaction. Quite logically, the response to being confronted with real physical danger, such as the appearance of a man-eating animal, would be to attack it or to escape from it. Whichever was the choice, the body would require instantly available energy, strength and concentration. There would be no time for slow deliberation or stages of progressive arousal, for by that time the adversary would be beginning its meal! If an appropriate response (fight or flight) to the stressor were forthcoming, then the biochemical and other changes triggered by the initial shock, would be utilized, and no ill-effects would be felt.

Today, people are seldom faced with such life and death stress situations. However, the mind and body may feel threatened in many other ways than by a man-eating tiger. Any perceived (accurately or not) threat or danger to the mind or body will produce a similar 'fight or flight' reaction, and there may be ways of producing an appropriate response to these. For instance, someone might say something which is perceived as being insulting and hurtful. The stress reaction, which includes a tensing of the muscles as well as biochemical (hormonal and other) changes, could simply be 'bottled up' and remain as an extra degree of muscular tension. If a suitable verbal and/or physical response were to be found, however, then again the preparation for action would have been expressed and used, and no ill-effects would result.

The degree of stress imposed on the body will vary with your perception of what constitutes a threat – one person would laugh and shrug off an insult, another would reach for a gun! It will also vary with your ability to respond appropriately. One might calmly but firmly state their views and inform the 'villain of the piece' of their feelings. Another might bluster and fluster and add fuel to the fire, and in doing so fail to obtain psychological release from the hurt and anger within. The stress factor, therefore, cannot be seen as the main determinant of the degree of 'fight or flight' reaction, but only as its potential trigger. The harm done to your body by prolonged, repeated arousal, is largely an outcome of your beliefs, attitudes, personality and ability to see objectively what constitutes real, and what constitutes imagined danger, physically or mentally.

The 'Chain Reaction' of Stress

The actual processes that take place during arousal and 'fight or flight' reactions are quite amazing to contemplate. It is possible to extrapolate these immediate changes and to see their potential for major physical damage if they are repeated or prolonged. The following process occurs instantly within the body in response to stress:

The muscles tense in preparation for activity; the hypothalamus (part of your brain) co-ordinates a number of hormonal changes; the pituitary gland is activated, and among other results of this is the production by the adrenal glands of the hormones, adrenaline and noradrenaline. As a result, a vast number of bodily changes occur; the pupils of the eye dilate – no doubt to see more clearly; the heart pumps more rapidly to service the extra requirements of the tense muscles, and this increases the blood pressure; the extra blood for the muscles requires extra oxygen, and the respiratory rate quickens to cope with this, as well as to help expel additional waste products resulting from increased activity. Blood being diverted to potential muscular activity requires the shut-down of some other functions, including reduction in blood through the kidneys, as well as the ceasing of digestive functions. To this end, saliva dries up and the intestines and stomach stop working. The body's need for additional energy is met by the liver releasing stored glucose into the bloodstream, where the oxygen changes it into readily available energy. In anticipation of extra activity, the skin cools the body down by opening its pores to encourage perspiration. Since blood is being diverted to the muscles, there is a tendency for the skin to become paler. There may be involuntary urination or defecation, due to an over-reaction of that part of the nervous system responsible for restoring the status quo (the parasympathetic nervous system); normally, however, the sphincters controlling these functions close to prevent any further activity until the crisis is past. Other aspects of the body's defence capability, the immune system, become less active during such arousal. This makes infection more likely at such a time. Since the muscles are tense, they will be producing lactic acid break-down products, which have the effect of reinforcing the anxiety and tension felt.

This listing of the chain reaction set up by stress is by no means fully comprehensive, but it gives an idea of what a devastating effect prolonged stress can have on normal body functions.

General Adaptation Syndrome

In the initial stages of arousal, most systems adapt to and accommodate such changes. After arousal there is a return to the status quo, especially if the response is adequate. However, if arousal is repeated over and over again, then some of the changes mentioned above stop being temporary and become chronic. The term employed to describe this process is the General Adaptation Syndrome (GAS). As your body adapts to repeated and constant stress factors, and as chronic symptoms become an accepted part of life, the general level of health declines. Such symptoms include headaches, dizziness, insomnia, blurred vision, swallowing difficulties, aching neck and shoulder muscles, high blood pressure, heart problems, circulatory problems, palpitations, asthma, allergies, indigestion, ulcers, back-ache, skin rashes, excessive sweating, colitis, sexual problems, depression, phobias and irritability.

Disturbances occur in the blood-sugar balance, giving rise to wild swings in energy levels and mood. If this is accompanied by the excessive use of sugar in the diet, and of stimulants such as tea, coffee and chocolate, the body's ability to maintain a normal blood-sugar level can be severely damaged. (Some researchers see this as a major cause of diabetes.) There is often a tendency to under-perform; self-doubt and insecurity become apparent, and there is a tendency for the defence mechanism to break down, making allergies and infections more likely. Personal relationships may become strained, libido often disappears, and all these changes lead to further anxiety and stress. A vicious circle of declining health, resulting from stress, is the bleak picture which is all too familiar in modern society.

Accompanied, as it often is, by poor nutrition, lack of exercise, and the debilitating habits of drinking (tea and coffee as well as alcohol) and smoking, the formula for disaster is well under way. Treatment by drugs and other medication results in nothing but a possible alteration of superficial symptoms. Indeed, by neglecting the underlying causes, symptomatic treatment may well do further harm. Masking and disguising a problem will never provide an answer to it.

This adaptation stage is critical in as much as most, if not all, of the symptoms are still reversible if the underlying stress factors are dealt with, and attention is paid to nutrition, exercise and structural integrity. How long this stage lasts depends upon many variables, including inherited factors, as well as the degree of stress, basic health habits, and the degree of emotional support available.

After a period of years (ten, twenty or more) the exhaustion stage of the GAS may be reached, and at this time the body simply ceases to be able to cope, and there is a collapse into one or other disease state. Break-down finally occurs, when even minor stress factors are not dealt with satisfactorily. At this point there may be collapse into a catastrophic illness, such as coronary heart disease, cancer, etc.

Knowledge of the signs and symptoms of stress, and of some of the ways in which the body copes with stress, can be seen as a necessary step towards understanding the enemy. Without being able to recognize and become aware of stress, it is possible to delude oneself that 'it just won't happen to me'.

The combination of prolonged stress and chronic fatigue has been put forward by some researchers (Drs Poteliakhof and Carruthers, in their report: *Real Health: the Ill Effects of Stress and their Prevention*) as a major factor in the cause of such conditions as rheumatoid arthritis, asthma and hypertension. Lack of sleep, persistent overwork and chronic anxiety is thought to result in hormonal imbalance, notably adrenal exhaustion or sluggishness. This is thought to interact with constitutional and inherited factors to determine the type of disease which develops.

Heart Disease

In the field of heart disease, research by Dr Peter Nixon at London's Charing Cross Hospital (detailed in *Stress and Relaxation* by Jane Madders) has shown contributory causes to be sustained and inappropriately high levels of arousal. This is mainly the result of the following factors, he suggests:

1. Pressures exerted by people from whom there is no escape.
2. Unacceptable time pressures, deadlines, etc.
3. Sleep deprivation.
4. A high score in the lifestyle changes list (see page 24).

Dr Nixon states that drugs are unsatisfactory in the

treatment of hypertension, since the underlying causes are not dealt with.

Neurological Disease

Among other stress-induced conditions are those that mimic more serious conditions. 'Symptoms suggesting serious neurological disease are common in patients suffering from anxiety states, or depressive illness, partly, or wholly, attributable to the effects of stress', states Dr Richard Godwin Austin, consultant neurologist of Nottingham General Hospital. 'The most common example seen in the neurological out-patient clinic is the patient suffering from recent onset headaches . . . Patients under physical or psychological stress, frequently develop tension headaches. These may occur in the setting of a depressive reaction, with symptoms of agitation or phobia. The headache often fails to respond to any form of simple analgesic.'

Cancer

There has also been a good deal of research into stress and its relationship to the onset of cancer. The German researcher Dr W. Herberger has noted that chronic anger, disappointment, fear and inability to cope with misfortune often play a role in its development. It has been found that the majority of cancer sufferers have a tendency to dwell on past misfortunes, real or imagined, and they have little sense of the future. Dr Hans Moolenburg, a noted Dutch physician, has described cancer patients as people who have been 'battered by fate'. It has also been noted that in the U.K., where six out of ten members of the general public acknowledge some belief in God or some spiritual agency, that nine out of ten cancer patients had no such belief. Cancer might therefore be described as, in part, a disease of 'spiritual deficiency'.

Load, Strain and Stress – Harmful and Helpful Factors

Before looking at some of the conclusions that have been come to concerning the relationship between personality traits and disease states, I want to touch on the possibly surprising healing potentials of some aspects of controlled stress. First, I want to be sure that you truly understand what is, and what is not stress.

Any reaction of your body or mind in response to an environmental or psychological demand is commonly termed a stress reaction. However, the total process of adaptation can be divided into three major phases, termed *load*, *strain* and *stress.*

Load is that part of the process in which an interaction takes place between you and any factor (physical, chemical or psychological) which is capable of disturbing you, or which demands a response from you. *Strain* is the term applied to the change(s) which result in your body/mind after the application of that load. It is the defensive (healing or normalizing) phase which follows on from the strain, in which an attempt is made to restore the situation to balance, which, strictly speaking, should be termed *stress.*

Stress can therefore often be seen to represent a positive, normalizing effort, something which can only be considered good, helpful and desirable. It is this self-healing process upon which we rely for survival, and in fact upon which all healing methods depend. For example, cut yourself (load and strain) and stress follows as the wound heals. This is homoeostasis in action.

Many other symptoms which we commonly try to 'cure'

are, in fact, nothing more than evidence of the body putting things right. One good example of this is that of the fever which occurs during an infection. The infecting agent (load) has led to local or general problems, leading in turn to a 'stress' reaction (adaptive response) on the part of the immune system, which involves elevation of the body's temperature (the fever). Under normal conditions this is a self-limiting process which causes no harm (except to the invading virus or bacteria) and which effectively gets rid of the infecting agent.

Such a stress reaction can actually be said to be life-saving, and yet – in many instances – the first objective of most people seems to be to try to over-ride this self-healing process and to take or do something to bring down the temperature! Such an action is clearly counterproductive, and not in the best interests of the body as a whole, unless the fever is of life-threatening proportions.

Stress as a Healing Factor?

There is yet another side to the concept of stress, and that is the therapeutic use of it (especially in alternative or complementary therapy) using the triple features of load, strain and response (stress). For example, manipulative methods such as chiropractic and osteopathy have historically seen as one of their primary roles the removal of obstructions to normal function as they normalize mechanical restrictions. They also understand that under ideal conditions self-normalizing responses take care of the processes of restoration of functional and structural integrity following appropriate manipulative care. What research has shown is that it is the degree of 'load' which the therapist applies which decides whether or not a good end-result is achieved by the treatment.

Selye's Evidence

In some of his early research, conducted in the 1930s, Hans Selye MD, demonstrated the homoeostatic process in action, with spectacular clarity. He observed, in experimental animals, a specific pattern of response to a variety of what he termed 'noxious stimuli'. Whether he used poisons of one sort or another, intense heat or cold, radiation or mechanical trauma (i.e. 'load'), he noted what he called a 'stress-syndrome' which involved, among other changes in adrenal and thymic activity and size, loss of weight, haemoconcentration, and sometimes intestinal ulceration. These changes are evidence of 'strain' and an inadequate 'stress' (self-healing) response, since where such problems had occurred, the homoeostatic mechanisms had clearly been overwhelmed and had failed to restore equilibrium – or health.

Selye made an important subsequent discovery following experiments in which the load factor involved the injection of noxious (poisonous) chemicals under the animal's skin. Selye, not surprisingly, observed a degree of response which was directly related to the concentration of the poison. He also noted that if a second stress factor (additional load) was then introduced (brief exposure to intense cold, heat, immobilization etc.) to animals previously exposed to mild degrees of toxicity there was an improvement of the initial response with, for example, reduction of tissue damage and speedy healing.

If, however, the initial toxic load had been heavily concentrated with very marked lesions, the secondary stressor (load) caused a rapid increase and spread of tissue damage, frequently leading to necrosis and death. This time the 'load' and 'strain' had overwhelmed the potential for healing.

These observations led Selye to state the truth which had been revealed. 'This was the crucial experiment showing that stress can either cure or aggravate a disease depending upon whether the inflammatory responses to a local irritant are necessary or superfluous.'

Selye attempted to make clear that a stress response involved many variable factors based on the unique and idiosyncratic ability of the organism (person or animal) to respond to load and strain. The variable nature of the response is based on genetic and acquired characteristics and energy reserves.

Whether treatment involves having something done to you (manipulation, insertion of an acupuncture needle, a change in diet, psychotherapy, taking a substance (whether a herb, a drug, a supplement or even a homoeopathic dilution of a substance) the same rules apply. It is always the body which is being 'asked' to respond, and this makes the potential healing response, by definition, a stress reaction.

Without any doubt it is the response of the individual which decides whether or not healing takes place, and that response (triggered by an appropriate therapeutic effort, or simply by innate self-healing mechanisms) is modulated (made stronger or weaker) by the current state of susceptibility, vitality or 'potential for response'.

This in turn depends upon what you or I were born with (genetic factors) and all the many things, good and bad, which have happened (acquired factors) since we were born. This, then, is the formula for assessing how well we can cope with any 'load'. You need to unravel a number of secrets.

● How susceptible or vital are you?
● How much can you do to improve things if you are susceptible, compromised or weakened?
● How much can you further build up your vital reserves?

These are key questions and have much to do with your current weaknesses and/or strengths in handling stress.

Arising from inherited and acquired characteristics is that

mysterious element known as 'personality', and many researchers have studied patterns of personality in relation to patterns of ill-health, with some surprising results.

Personality of the Cancer Patient

Carl Simonton MD is one of the world's leading researchers into the effect of the mind on the development of and recovery from cancer, and here is what he said in 1978:

'To summarize what I consider the salient points from the literature and my own experience in working in these areas for four years now, the biggest single factor that I can find as a predisposing factor to the actual development of the disease is the loss of a serious love object, occurring six to eighteen months prior to the diagnosis. This is well documented in several long-term studies. Now, the significant thing about this is that obviously not everyone who undergoes a serious loss, such as a loss of a spouse or a child, develops a malignancy or any other serious disease. That's only one factor. The loss, whether real or imagined, has to be very significant; and even more important is the feeling that it engenders in the patient. The loss has to be such, and the response to the loss such, that it engenders the feeling of helplessness and hopelessness. Therefore, it's more than a loss – it's the culmination of the life-history pattern of the patient. And this also is well defined in the literature.

'I believe the work that has come out in *Type-A Behaviour and Your Heart* (Friedman and Rosenman, 1975), shows clearly that there is a life-history pattern in the development of heart disease, and I believe that, if we continue to look, we will find predisposing psychological factors in the development of all diseases. Those predisposing factors most agreed upon as (negative) personality characteristics of the cancer patient are:

1. A great tendency to hold resentment and a marked inability to forgive.
2. A tendency toward self-pity.
3. A poor ability to develop and maintain meaningful, long-term relationships.
4. A very poor self-image.'

As you will see in the final chapter on the healing power of the mind, an enormous amount of help to cancer patients has been derived by the simple measure of deep relaxation and positive mental imagery. Stress is undoubtedly a major factor in much chronic and acute illness and, if this is so, then any intelligent individual should be able to work out that reversing the stressful input will help considerably towards restoring health. Even more obvious is the fact that by becoming aware of these facts, and by reducing and eliminating stress factors, together with a general stress-proofing programme, prevention of ill health will be greatly enhanced.

There is a school of thought which holds that the attitude and psychological patterns of the individual will determine what patterns disease takes. Examples of this work, taken from 'Specific Relations of Attitude to Psychological Change' by P. T. and F. K. Graham, University of Wisconsin Medical School, 1961, are as follows:

Symptom	Attitude
Nausea and vomiting	This person feels something wrong has happened and probably feels responsible. He wishes it had not happened, and wishes he could undo it. He wishes things were the way they were before. He wishes he had not done it.
Psoriasis	This person feels something constantly gnawing at him and that he has to put up with it.

Symptom	Attitude
Asthma	This person feels left out in the cold and wants to shut the person or situation out. He feels unloved, rejected, disapproved of, shut out, and he wishes not to deal with the person or situation. He wishes to blot it, or him out and not to have anything to do with it or him.
Eczema	This person feels he is being frustrated and can do nothing about it. He feels interfered with, blocked, prevented from doing something; he feels unable to make himself understood.
Constipation	This person feels he is in a situation from which nothing could come, but keeps on with it grimly. He feels things will never get any better but has to stick with it.
Migraine	This person feels something has to be achieved and relaxes after the effort. He has to accomplish something, is driving himself, striving. He has to get things done. A goal has to be reached, then he lets down and stops driving himself.
Rheumatoid arthritis	This person feels tied down and wants to get free. He feels restrained, restricted, confined, and wants to be able to move around.

Symptom	Attitude
Diarrhoea	This person sees himself faced with a meaningful task and wishes it were over or done with. He wishes impending events were behind him.

(The full list can be found in *Health for the Whole Person*, Westview Press, Boulder, CO, 1981).

CHAPTER 3

The Musculoskeletal System and Stress

The body and the mind can often be shown to reflect their respective current states of health. In this chapter I explain the phenomenon of 'armouring', in which the body directly takes on the stresses of the mind in a physical form, which can be felt by both the person involved and any therapist with palpatory skills.

There is another dimension to the way in which stress influences health, to be found in the research conducted over the past 40 years by Professor Irvin Korr into dysfunction of spinal regions as part of the 'organizer' of the processes of disease. Stress of a psychological or emotional nature can produce marked changes in the musculoskeletal system, profoundly influencing the overall functioning of the body. All emotional changes are mirrored in the soft tissues. Attitudes such as anger or fear, as well as moods such as excitement or depression, produce muscular postures and patterns. There is also a close link between habitual posture and psychological attitudes and states.

Many postures and defensive tensions arise from anxiety and stress. If this is continued and repeated, restrictions and alterations will take place in the soft tissues. If unreleased, these become self-perpetuating, and the source of pain and further stress. The ability to relax is frequently lost, and the consequent drain on nervous energy is marked.

Have you ever focused sunlight through a magnifying glass to obtain a pin-point of heat? If, in this analogy, the light of the sun, represents stress in all its myriad forms, then the focusing mechanism (the lens) represents the nervous system. Attention must be paid to all aspects of this phenomenon, the stress factors, and how to avoid or minimize them, the body systems which deal with stress and, in particular, the nervous system, which to a large extent determines how the body will cope with it. No two people react to stress in the same way. Even under identical conditions, reactions and effects will vary. While it is important to know what stress is, and how the body reacts to it in general, attention should also be paid to the individual receiving the stress, the unique characteristics of whom will determine the end result.

Why does one person develop an ulcer, another diabetes and yet another high blood pressure? All these conditions might be the apparent result of similar stress patterns. It can be assumed, therefore, that the stress factors do not themselves determine the response of the body. The unique make-up and history of an individual is the determining factor in deciding just what aspect of the body will adapt or react in response to any stimulus or stress. Disease, in the final analysis, is the failure on the part of the body to adapt to or cope with the demands placed upon it by the total environment in which it lives. This includes demands of a stressful nature, whether internally generated or externally applied.

The Nervous System and Spinal Dysfunction

What is it that determines which aspect of the body will break down under prolonged stress? There are inherited tendencies, of course, and these must be borne in mind. As already mentioned, there is another key 'organizer' within the body, to which the osteopathic profession, in particular, pays much attention. This is the nervous system and the role played by the nervous system and spinal dysfunction in affecting the way in which particular patterns of ill health are shown. Professor Korr has established:

1. That there exists in most people's spines, areas or segments, which are abnormal or aberrant, in one of (at least) three ways. These areas may be hypersensitive to pressure, restricted in mobility (movement) or asymmetrical (out of position). Such changes are common, even in apparently healthy people.
2. These areas are abnormal in the degree of tension or tone that is present in the local soft tissues, and the nerves in such areas respond abnormally to any stimulus. Some of the nerve centres which deal with messages of sensation, or which direct automatic function or voluntary function, will as a result, be in a state of chronic over-excitability. In other words, they will react more rapidly and more strongly, and for longer than they should, in response to even a mild stimulus of any sort (emotional or physical).
3. This state of over-reaction is often manifested in the tissues or organs which these nerve structures supply or control.

These abnormally reacting segments may result from injury or postural stress, or they may result from problems in a particular organ or system (say a diseased gall-bladder), which feeds back 'irritable' messages along the nerves supplying it to the spinal centres where local irritation may become chronic and cause changes in the tone of the local soft tissue. Whether the initial cause is reflex (from the organ to the spinal area) or direct (i.e. biomechanical changes in the spine itself), the result is an over-reacting segment of the nervous system.

Constant Over- (or Under) Stimulation

Since the nervous system organizes the body's adaptive and protective functions in dealing with all environmental variations and extremes (changes of temperature, increased activity, etc.) as well as its reaction to emotional stress (alarm reaction, etc.), such a state of over-excitability in a particular area has enormous local and distant consequences.

For example, instead of an organ being controlled in a balanced harmonious way, it might be kept in a state of near constant over- (or under-) stimulation because the nerve centres controlling its function are in this condition. Such an area is known as a *facilitated* segment (i.e. it allows easier conduction of nerve impulses and activity). If such an area occurs in the upper spinal region, it might be associated, for example, with heart dysfunction. A definite pattern of spinal lesion has been found in most cases of angina pectoris. If, in a mid-spinal area, then the effect might be on the digestive organs, such as the liver or pancreas. Now, it must be remembered that although the spinal area is maintaining such over- or under- activity via the nervous system, the problem might have originated in the organ itself for a variety of reasons (infection, toxic state, etc.), and the spinal irritation and consequent 'facilitated state' might, originally, have resulted from this.

If stress is part of your life, then the presence in the spine of such areas – and they are the rule rather than the exception – will cause over-reaction in a chronic manner, and the end result will be that the target organ or system will become abnormal in its function. After a while, if unchecked, this will result in damage and dysfunction of the affected organ, and disturbance of the entire body function. Osteopathic methods enable practitioners to speedily identify such 'facilitated' or lesioned segments. Osteopathic manipulation of the spine and soft tissues (e.g. neuromuscular technique) can often normalize these areas, but in chronic cases only limited improvement may be possible.

The Effect of Psychological Stress on the Body

Let's look at what happens when psychological stress impacts with our physical bodies. First, chemical changes take place in which there is increased production in the brain of substances such as serotonin, epinephrine and many other neurotransmitters, some of which dramatically increase the excitability of nerve cells. Along with this, in response to internally produced hormonal substances, comes heightened metabolic activity, and at the same time muscular changes occur, with consequent postural alteration (hunched shoulders for example).

If such muscular tensions are held for more than a short time there occurs a reduction in blood flow through the affected tissues, leading to a combined lessening throughput of fresh oxygenated blood, as well as a poorer drainage effort, leaving waste products relatively stationary. Excessive levels of calcium, lactic acid and various other acids then build up which further increases the tendency towards 'tightening', and increased sensitivity of local nerve tissues.

Eventually these changes – less oxygen and more toxic waste products – produce discomfort or pain, and reduce energy output (the musculoskeletal system is the body's main user of energy) leading to even further muscle contraction and chronic dysfunction.

Symptoms such as pain, stiffness, mal-co-ordination and cramp may all be displayed, along with a good deal of tiredness, as energy is wasted on unnecessary muscular tension. Once pain itself becomes a feature, a self-perpetuating cycle develops, creating more tension, and ultimately more pain.

Overuse, Misuse and Abuse

A wide variety of stressors can be involved in this all too common scenario, including emotional, occupational, habitual, postural, traumatic and congenital factors. All these can generally be included in the umbrella terms 'overuse, misuse or abuse'. The progression can be summarized by saying that stress (when poorly handled) causes changes in the soft tissues (muscles etc.) and that the changes themselves then produce more stress.

The effects of these changes on various vital functions, such as breathing, are all too common. One recent study (*Journal of Psychosomatic Research*, Vol. 31, pages 215-21) described a survey of causes relating to 69 consecutive patients, under the age of 40, brought to an emergency care unit suffering from acute chest pain, who were found not to have any organic disease such as heart or lung problems.

The results showed that a common feature of the men (36 out of the 69) was their Type A behaviour (see pages 30 and 80), whereas the women fell into categories which were labelled 'neurotic' often displaying 'vital exhaustion' (chronic fatigue). A major feature in many of these people was a high score on the 'life event' schedule (see page 24), a tendency towards hyperventilation (see page 103) along with palpable tension in the chest muscles.

This is a classic illustration of the way in which poor stress coping leads to structural changes (tense muscles etc.) and ultimately functional problems (hyperventilation and breathing as well as swallowing difficulties) leading on to acute pain.

A further study on this increasingly common response to stress was described in 1989 (*Journal of Psychosomatic Research*, Vol. 33, pages 393-406) in which the same series of interlocking features were noted, leading to the conclusion that there are multi-causal features acting in these people, some clearly physical (muscle tension) and others clearly psychological (anxiety etc.), all intertwined with behavioural and habitual features.

The answer to all this is to change the way we deal with stress, and to avoid unnecessary exposure to it where possible. Both strategies require understanding of the way we react to stress, and the many ways available for reducing its negative effects.

Wilhelm Reich – An Early Pioneer

An early researcher into the physical changes induced by poor stress coping was the controversial medical giant Wilhelm Reich. Having started out his career at the turn of the century as a mainstream follower of Freud, he gradually evolved his own way of understanding the human condition. His belief was that when tension states existed, they showed either in the form of what he termed 'character (psychological) armouring' or 'muscular (physiological) armouring'.

He did not accept that the physical changes resulted from the psychological, nor the reverse (both positions being strongly argued by factions within medicine). Rather he held to the view that 'muscular attitudes (bodily states) and character attitude (psychological states) have the same function . . . they can replace one another and be influenced by one another. Basically they cannot be separated.'

In treatment, when he found resistance in treating the mind, he switched to an approach which dealt with the physical manifestations of this interaction, and vice versa. A system of treatment based on Reich's pioneering work is currently practised widely, and is known as bioenergetics.

Kathleen Sandman, writing in 1984 in the *Journal of Manipulative and Physiological Therapeutics* (Vol 7, pages 237-41) insists that psychological and physiological factors are synergistic (interacting and interdependent), and that we cannot consider one without the other if we are to successfully understand how stress affects us, and what we can do about it.

Different psychological states produce quite varied musculoskeletal effects. For example, the frontalis muscle on the head is one of the most affected and reactive muscles when you are depressed, in contrast to the extensor muscles of the arm which are most affected when you are agitated or anxious.

Three 'Fists'

On a wider level Reich proposed seven areas of cross-restriction (pelvis, diaphragm etc.) which were identifiable in response to particular forms of emotional disturbance and which were amenable to treatment. British osteopath Philip Latey has concentrated these areas into just three 'fists' (metaphor for clenched fists, in response to long-held emotional distress).

These are the upper fist (head-neck region), the middle fist (chest-diaphragm region) and the lower fist (pelvic region), palpation and observation of which allow the trained therapist to 'read' the emotional stress patterns of the patient as they have become cemented into his/her pattern of posture and use.

Release of the physical tensions is part of the normalization process needed to correct the underlying stress patterns (something which also requires counsel-ling), increased self-awareness, and ultimately enhanced coping skills so that the whole problem does not reappear soon after therapy.

Whatever the mechanical, physical and psychological involvement, it must now be apparent that stress is more than just a nuisance. Chapter 5 deals with methods of assessing your level of stress, and looks at the process of stress reduction and stress-proofing. For, if taken in hand, there is the potential for a return to a real state of health, and with it the chance to live life to the full, rather than spiralling downwards into an inevitable physical or mental collapse. How can you recognize to what extent stress is currently affecting your health level and potential? To find out, use the checklists in Chapter 5.

CHAPTER 4

The Healing Power of Hardiness, Happiness and Self-Esteem

The self-healing processes of the body depend upon a healthy immune system and, as already explained, this complicated array of defensive capabilities (for the immune system is not a single entity, but rather a collection of interacting elements) is under the direct control of the mind.

The implications of this mind-immune system connection (studied in medicine as psychoneuroimmunology) are tremendous, especially when it is discovered that where a person's mind has habitually (possibly through learned responses) affected their immune system for the worse, they can often be taught to alter negative and unhelpful patterns of thought and to start to adopt positive, health-enhancing ones.

The Hardiness Factor

I have already touched briefly on the idea of a cluster of personality characteristics known as the 'hardiness factor' (see pages 10 and 29), as well as 'self-esteem' (page 32). In this chapter I explore this territory more deeply, and describe other aspects of the positive concept of self-esteem as a health/immune system booster, and the negative 'fall-out' from attitudes of cynicism and poor self-image.

Established knowledge now tells us that our mind controls our immune system – that complex of interacting systems and substances which defends our body not just against external invasion, but also against self-generated attacks, such as cancer. It is therefore of more than passing importance that we understand just how attitudes and personality traits can influence our defensive capacity.

Norman Cousins, author of the book *Anatomy of an Illness* (Bantam, 1987), and adjunct professor of psychiatry at UCLA School of Medicine, writing in the Journal of the *American Holistic Medical Association*, tells us that in the early 1980s he had asked colleagues at the Brain Research Institute for a listing of known secretions produced in the brain. He received a list of 34 substances, some of which allowed the body to alleviate pain (endorphins) and others which helped the body combat infection (such as interleukin 2), whilst others had different immune-enhancing functions.

Writing in 1986 he states: 'Today they don't even dare count the number of brain secretions. The brain can combine sub-units available to it into an almost infinite number of substances . . . in some instances it can secrete and "prescribe" substances far more helpful than any drugs. *But, under circumstances of fear, panic, pain, exasperation or rage, it is extremely difficult for the brain to produce the appropriate substances.'*

It was the father of medicine, Hippocrates, who pronounced, over two thousand years ago, that *'it is the body which is the physician of its own diseases'*, and Cousins's question: 'If negative emotions like panic can create disease, what is the role of positive emotions – love, hope, faith, laughter, playfulness, creativity?' is an echo of that earlier holistic concept. Cousins concluded that such positive emotions protect against anxiety and despair; that it is not possible to entertain two contrary feelings at the same time, and that positive emotions drive out negative ones. He ascribes the 'miracles' of Lourdes – examples of very real spontaneous healing of serious illness – to the healing effects of the patients' faith and love. In effect, such people become 'programmed' to live rather than die.

Dr Bernie Siegel, author of the international bestseller *Love, Medicine and Miracles* (Rider, 1987), who is a surgeon, physician and inspirational teacher, has focused on the phenomenon of *self-induced healing and what he calls 'the physiology of optimism'*. He records that he has seen patients die rapidly when a physician's inappropriate words have 'sentenced' the patient to death. He has also seen how, under anaesthetic, the body responds to positive suggestions to stop bleeding, or to correct heart irregularities. 'How do the body and mind act as a unit?', he asks. By having an internal sixth sense (the immune system) over which the mind has complete and absolute control.

He urges patients to become responsible participants in their healing; not by the introduction of false hope, but by giving themselves and their healing (immune) systems all the 'love and live' messages they can. He asks them to keep a journal of their feelings and dreams; to sit regularly in front of a mirror and to verbalize self-affirming statements; to share their feelings and let their immune system know that they are reaching out for help; to live one hour at a time; to join therapy groups which meet at least weekly, where they are counselled and loved . . . All these elements have been shown to boost immune function.

Placebo Power

Without realizing it, almost all physicians, of whatever school, use the healing powers of the mind through activation of what is known as the placebo effect. In medicine a placebo is commonly thought of as a 'dummy' substance (coloured water or a sugar pill, for example) which is used to treat someone when a regular medicine is thought inappropriate, or which is used in clinical studies to compare its effects with 'real' treatment or drugs. In reality, a placebo's definition alters, depending upon how it is used. For example, sometimes the doctor knows the substance or method is a placebo, but the patient does not know (this is called a known placebo); in other instances neither the doctor nor the patient is aware of this (double blind placebo). Some placebos have a definite effect (such as causing a mild flushing) while having no relevance to the condition being treated. This 'active' placebo is therefore more powerful than an inactive one, because the patient is aware that 'something' is happening. The opposite would be an inactive placebo, something totally inert and unable to cause any changes in the patient's system.

In all cases, however, if a substance is given to a patient with therapeutic intent, whether or not it has any biochemical potential to do anything at all in the body, some changes occur, usually for the better (when they are for the worse the substance is called a nocebo rather than a placebo). And, amazingly, the more the practitioner giving the substance believes it to be useful, the greater the beneficial placebo result.

It has even been found that different coloured placebos affect different conditions. For examples, green tablets improve anxiety conditions more than placebos of other colours; yellow helps depression; blue is more sedative, and pink more stimulating. Overall, placebo injections are more effective than those taken by mouth.

How Much Effect Can Placebos Have?

The answer to this is that placebos can have an enormous effect. When compared with the pain-killing effects of powerful morphine drugs, dummy placebos showed themselves capable of achieving 56% as much relief from pain. Many studies have been carried out which show placebo medication/treatment to have been effective in cases as divergent as anorexia, depression, dermatitis, diarrhoea, stomach pain, hallucinations, headache, palpitations, weakness and many others.

If such a degree of healing or relief can be seen when dummy substances are taken, then the benefits seen from taking regular medication must also have an element of placebo effect. This means that when 'real' treatment achieves its benefits, at least some (probably a large degree) of the credit should go to the placebo effect; which is another way of saying that credit should go to the self-healing powers of the immune system. This is why we should be concerned with this odd by-way of medicine, since it helps us to understand just how powerful are the immune functions which hope can trigger, for this surely is why placebos work.

Belief that something will help is the starting point, and the dummy (or real) medication the focus. The result is an improved state of health, not falsely achieved, but through the innate self-healing potentials of the body becoming harnessed to the task in hand. Our attitudes and emotions can both help or hinder this process, whether or not a placebo, or 'real' treatment is involved.

This subject is discussed at length by Peter Bennett in *The Textbook of Natural Medicine* (Bastyr College, Seattle, 1988) who suggests that the key to liberating this enormous healing potential in a doctor/patient setting should involve treatment which does no harm; a search for the causes of the health problem; a nurturing of the doctor/patient relationship; *cultivation of faith, hope and expectation*, the exploring of the healing process as a learning process, as well as exploration of the value of what he (Bennett) calls altered states of consciousness (hypnosis, self-hypnosis, deep relaxation, meditation and visualization). These concepts seem close enough to those of Cousins and Siegel to be very much related, and to be well worth looking at in the setting of stress reduction.

If you *know* that in a state of deep relaxation/meditation you can guide your mind to healing and health-enhancing images, and that these do have very real benefits to offer you, your enthusiasm and expectation will be increased. This is not a false hope, but a certainty that your immune system will function more efficiently. If, at the same time, the causes of any health problems are being safely dealt with you have a powerful combination with which to promote optimal health or recovery.

A Review of Psychoneuroimmunology

George Solomon, writing in *Advance,* the journal of the Institute for the Advancement of Health (Winter 1985, pages 6-19) investigated the connection between the central nervous system and immune function. He summarizes his initial thoughts (some of which are now substantiated by further research) as follows:

1. The way we cope with life (stress) and our personalities influences how susceptible we are to disease by the influence on our immune function. This has been proved in numerous human and animal studies which show that when our psychological defences are weakened (poor 'hardiness'), and we have a physical predisposition, disease becomes more likely.

2. Emotional upsets and distress can alter the course of any disease. This, too, has been proved to be true. For example, in cases where people with rheumatoid arthritis, with poor psychological defences, show a more rapid progression of the disease than those with better coping skills (remember that coping skills can be

enhanced by careful counselling and psychotherapy). Hardiness protects against ill-health.

3. Severe emotional disturbances are usually accompanied by a decline in immune competence. This is known to be true following extensive evaluation of features of the immune system in specific emotional states (such as depression).

4. Deliberately engineered or naturally occurring stress has a negative effect on immune function. The argument is offered at times that the emotional state could well be the result rather than the cause of immune depression, and Solomon, on examining this, has shown that it is indeed stress which brings about the immune decline, rather than the opposite. Human grief and bereavement is a common example of this phenomenon.

5. Sometimes this works in reverse, and psychological disturbance follows on from severe immune disease. This has been observed in some cases of AIDS and some auto-immune diseases such as lupus erythematosus.

6. Experimental alterations to the central nervous system affects immune function. Studies show this to be true: for example, when parts of the brain are damaged, specific aspects of immune function decline in efficiency (posterior hypothalamus damage makes allergies more intense, for example).

7. Methods which enhance psychological function (relaxation techniques, psychotherapy, hypnosis etc.) should be able to enhance immune function. It has been proved that a 'distress-free' state of mind, brought about by such therapies, results in marked immune function enhancement.

The Work of C. Norman Shealy and Caroline Myss

To round out the concepts described in this chapter, here are the conclusions arrived at by C. Norman Shealy, famed holistic physician, neurosurgeon and founder of the American Holistic Medical Association, and Caroline Myss, inspirational intuitive lecturer on the theme of human consciousness, and explained in their book *The Creation of Health* (Stillpoint, 1988).

They noted a pattern of eight different, yet often overlapping, stress features from which much physical disease derives, through crises in emotional, psychological and spiritual well-being.

1. Deeply consuming emotional, psychological or spiritual stress which remains unresolved. Such stress might be traced back to childhood (feelings of rejection or inadequacy, for example) or might result from recent life crises (loss of job, death of a spouse, for example).
2. The holding of negative beliefs which strongly influence the way we respond to life emotionally.
3. An inability to show or accept love, one of our greatest needs, which is often deficient in modern society.
4. A lack of a sense of humour, accompanied by an inability to see the difference between what is serious and what is not.
5. A lack of a sense of control or empowerment. This is very much the 'control' feature of the hardiness factor I described earlier in this chapter. The surrender of control to others, leading to a sense of dependency and powerlessness is a common feature in seriously ill people. Recovery is often seen when the individual regains an effective voice in the way they live their life, and the choices which are made.
6. A strong degree of caring about oneself, as shown by how much care is taken over matters such as diet, exercise, use of addictive substances etc. This is very much linked to how we feel about ourselves – self-respect and sense of self-worth.
7. A lack of a sense of purpose and meaning; with emotions such as despair, depression, worthlessness all

contributing to the progression towards ill health.

8. A feature called denial, in which the challenges facing the individual are not faced, but are instead denied. An example is the smoker, already in a state of declining health, who refuses to acknowledge the damage caused by the habit, or even to contemplate stopping.

It is through the involvement of these patterns that we directly participate in the creation of our own state of health or ill-health, say Shealy and Myss.

So, what are the lessons to be learned from this and other examples of the explosion of research and investigation into the mind/body link and the connection between our emotions and our state of health?

- That a healthy immune system goes together with a hardy personality to provide the basis for a healthy life.
- That we can modify our stress-coping abilities if we wish to, and that this can dramatically encourage healing and health.
- That the techniques described in this book offer a basis for achieving this goal.

A combination of stress reduction (avoiding the obvious – see next chapter for questionnaires to guide you on this) together with improved defences against stress (relaxation, meditation techniques, enhanced 'hardiness features' etc.) provides the perfect balance of practical methods which can lead to a happier, healthier future.

You should now spend some time evaluating just how well your stress-coping skills are operating, as well as having a good look at the stresses in your life, so that positive action can stem from the knowledge gained.

CHAPTER 5

Assessing Your Stress

Before looking at ways in which it is possible to start reducing the degree of stress in your life it is as well to have a clear idea of how much is already present and active. You should assess both your current level of short-term anxiety (if any), and any underlying anxiety there might be. The first will give clues to what in your attitudes and everyday life may need adjusting, and the second will indicate whether or not there may be a need for professional guidance or counselling.

It is also helpful to review signs and symptoms to try to establish just what stress is doing to you at this moment. Reference to the 'changes in lifestyle' list on page 24 will give a guide to the current level of stress to which you are exposed. Remember that a high score on this list indicates a high risk of illness. The actual determining factor, however, is yourself. In this regard, the potential for stress affecting you will be greater if you are already in a high state of arousal engendered by particular personality traits. A further series of predisposing factors may arise from your eating habits, exercise (or lack of it), etc., and this will also, to some extent, be assessable by answering some of the following checklists.

There are no absolute right and wrong answers in most

of these lists. What is being sought is recognition of where you are now in relation to stress, and in relation to your own unique potential for achieving optimum high-level health. By following the advice given in later chapters, there is a virtual certainty that, in rechecking in, say, six months' time, a much rosier picture would emerge.

1. *Is stress currently affecting you physically?*

Tick 'yes' (✓) if the answer applies more than once weekly. If monthly, answer 'sometimes' (±), and if less frequently than monthly, answer 'no' (✗).

Is your sleep disturbed by any of the
   following?:   (✓) (±) (✗)
(a) difficulty in getting to sleep
(b) waking frequently in the night
(c) waking in the early hours, unable to
    sleep again
Are you experiencing sexual difficulties?
   (impotence, lack of desire for sex, etc.)
Do you have difficulty in sitting still
   without fidgeting?
Do you have headaches?
Do you bite your nails?
Do you feel unusually tired?
Do you have frequent indigestion, such
   as heartburn?
Do you crave for food other than at
   mealtimes?
Do you have no appetite at mealtimes?
Is bowel function erratic – sometimes
   constipated, sometimes very loose?
Do you sweat for no obvious reason?
Do you have any 'tics', such as touching
   the face, hair, moustache etc.
   repeatedly?
Do you frequently feel nauseous?

(✓) (±) (✗)

Do you ever faint or have dizzy spells
   without obvious cause?
Do you feel breathless and tight-chested
   when not exerting yourself?
Do you cry or feel the desire to cry?
Are you suffering from high blood
   pressure?
Do you feel obliged to take a drink to
   'unwind'?
Do you smoke to calm your nerves?

If you answer 'yes' to two or more of these questions (two
'sometimes' answers are equal to one 'yes') then, almost
certainly, your body is adapting to stress, and it is time to
take appropriate action. In the absence of organic disease,
all such symptoms are remediable by the measures
outlined in the chapters to follow.

Note: Some of the above symptoms can arise from other
(e.g. nutritional) causes, but usually these are combined
with stress factors.

2. *Is stress currently affecting you mentally?*

(✓) (±) (✗)

Do you lack interest in life?
Do you feel helpless and unable to cope?
Are you irritable without obvious cause?
Are you frequently aware of being afraid
   of disease?
Do you feel yourself to be a failure?
Do you dislike yourself?
Do you find making up your mind
   difficult?
Are you disinterested in other people?
Is it difficult to show your true feelings?

(✓) (±) (✗)

Do you feel suppressed (i.e. unexpressed)
  anger?

Do you feel your appearance has altered
  for the worse?

Is it difficult to relax and laugh?

Do you feel yourself a victim of other
  people's dislike or animosity?

Do you feel you are neglected, or have
  been let down?

Do you feel you have 'failed' in your role
  as parent, spouse, child?

Do you have a fear of what the future
  holds?

Do you feel no one understands you?

Do you feel isolated and that there is no
  one to turn to?

Do you find it difficult to concentrate?

Do you find it difficult to complete one
  job properly before rushing on to the
  next?

Do you fear enclosed or open spaces?

Do you feel uncomfortable in touching
  and being touched?

If you answer 'yes' to three or more of these questions (two
'sometimes' answers equal one 'yes'), then you probably
are emotionally affected by stress, and action should be
taken as outlined in the chapters that follow. See these
signs as a warning and a challenge to be met by personal
effort. If, on this and the previous list, a combined total of
five or more 'yes' answers were given, then it might be
advisable to seek professional advice as well as undertaking
the health-building, stress-reducing and stress-proofing
programmes.

Anxiety Tendency Checklist

You may have had low scores on the previous checklists, and yet have a tendency towards future problems. Dr Charles Spielberger, Professor of Psychology at the University of South Florida, has given the following shortened anxiety 'trait' self-evaluation scale:

'Read each statement and then circle the appropriate number that indicates how you generally feel. There are no right or wrong answers. Do not spend too much time on any one statement, but give the answer which seems to describe how you generally feel. Add up the eight numbers you have circled to obtain your score.

	Almost never	Some- times	Often	Almost always
I feel nervous and restless	1	2	3	4
I feel satisfied with myself	4	3	2	1
I feel that difficulties are piling up so that I cannot overcome them	1	2	3	4
I feel a failure	1	2	3	4
I have disturbing thoughts	1	2	3	4
I lack self-confidence	1	2	3	4
I feel secure	4	3	2	1
I worry too much over something that really does not matter	1	2	3	4

Only five per cent of the population has a score of 10 or less. Half the population has a score of around 15. Only five per cent of the population has a score of over 20.'

This gives you a guide to whether your current attitudes are likely to bring you a stressful future. The advice and exercises given in subsequent chapters should enable you to drastically reduce your score if you carry them out diligently for some months. This, and the previous checklists, can become the yardstick by which you measure the success of your self-help programme.

Type A and B Personality Checklist

Drs Meyer Friedman and Ray Rosenmann have found that certain personality types are more prone to coronary heart disease, and that it is possible for these types to modify their behaviour, and by doing so to reduce their tendency to such disease.

Type A people are three times more prone to heart attacks than Type B. If half or more of the Type A characteristics apply to you, then you belong to this category and should seriously consider modifying your behaviour patterns and lifestyle. Even three or four Type A characteristics would indicate some inherent stress, and should be modified.

Type A	*Type B*
Very competitive	Not competitive (at work or play)
Strong, forceful personality	Easy-going or retiring
Does things quickly	Methodical or slow in doing things
Strives for promotion at work, or social advancement	Content with present position at work and socially
Wants public recognition	No desire for public recognition
Angered easily by events and people	Slow to anger
Restless when not active	Enjoys periods of idleness
Speaks rapidly	Speaks slowly
Seems to thrive on doing more than one thing at a time	Happiest doing one thing at a time

Type A	*Type B*
Walks, gesticulates and eats quickly	Walks, gesticulates and eats without rushing
Impatient at any delay	Patient and not upset by delay
Very conscious of time; enjoys having to meet deadlines	Not time-conscious; ignores deadlines
Always arrives on time	Often late
Taut facial muscles and often clenches fists	Relaxed facial muscles and does not clench fists

Modification is achieved by selecting a particular characteristic and deliberately trying to copy the opposite, Type B, characteristic. For example, the quick eater should allow more time to eat and chew more slowly, until this has become habitual. One by one, all Type A activities can be reduced, or even totally altered.

Nutritional Checklist

The aim of this is to assess whether or not you have an adequate sense of what is and what is not desirable with regard to nutrition. Guidelines to what constitutes an 'anti-stress' diet will be given in the next chapter.

In the meantime, check your rating by ticking 'yes' (✓) for daily, 'sometimes' (±) for no more than once a week, and 'no' (X) for less than once a week.

(✓) (±) (✗)

Do you eat refined (i.e. white) flour products?
Do you include sugar (any colour) in your diet?

Do you drink tea, coffee, chocolate or   (✓) (±) (✗)
cola drinks?

Do you drink alcohol, other than the
equivalent of 1.5 glasses wine or 1 pint
of beer daily?

Do you eat foods containing any chemical
additives (colouring, flavouring etc.)?

Do you skip meals?

Do you pick at food between meals?

Do you eat more than 6oz (150g) of
animal protein daily?

Do you eat convenience, ready-made
(junk) foods e.g. instant mashed
potato, TV dinners, or tinned foods?

Do you add salt to your food?

Do you eat fried or highly seasoned and
spiced foods?

Do you eat fatty meats, smoked or
preserved foods?

Do you eat fresh fruit?

Do you eat salad?

Do you insist on fresh vegetables only?

Do you use herbs for flavouring food?

Do you ensure adequate fibre in your
diet?

Do you eat whole cereal products (such
as brown rice and wholemeal bread)?

Do you drink herb teas?

Do you take a multivitamin or
multimineral supplement?

Do you eat non-animal proteins, such as
seeds, nuts, pulses?

Do you eat breakfast?

Do you eat natural yogurt?

Do you believe that what you eat affects
your health in a major way for good or
ill?

The first 12 questions should be answered 'no' (X). The second 12 should be answered 'yes' (✓) or 'sometimes' (±). Modified eating, to the pattern that would provide these answers, would dramatically alter the ability of your body to cope with stress and to operate at a higher level of well-being.

Deficiency Checklist

To assess whether or not you are deficient in particular nutritional substances, check the following signs:

Are your nails ridged?
Do your nails break easily?
Do you have white flecks in your nails?
Do your gums bleed when you clean your teeth?
Do you get frequent mouth ulcers?
Do you have stretch marks in your skin?
Do you get cracks in the corners of your mouth?
Does strong light irritate you?
Are your eyes, mouth or nose dry?
Have you lost your sense of taste or smell?
Do you get cramp?
Does your skin scale or flake?
Do you have a strong body odour?
Do your feet smell strongly?
Do you bruise easily?
Do you recall your dreams on waking?

All of these *might* result from nutritional deficiencies – there could be other reasons, of course. If you have a number of positive answers, then you are probably suffering from clinical deficiency in one or more substances. It is worth noting that all nutritional substances (vitamins, minerals, enzymes, trace elements, etc.) are required by the body for optimum function. Any deficiency will have effects on all body systems and functions.

Lifestyle and Exercise Checklist

Advice regarding this aspect of health maintenance and stress reduction will be found in the following chapters. This checklist is to be used as a means of increasing awareness as to desirable and undesirable habitual patterns in everyday life.

(✓) (±) (✗)

Do you work more than 5½ days weekly?

Do you work more than 10 hours on a work day?

Do you take less than half an hour for each main meal?

Do you eat quickly and not chew thoroughly?

Do you smoke?

Do you get less than seven hours sleep each night?

Do you listen to relaxing music?

Do you practice daily relaxation or meditation?

Do you take 30 minutes exercise at least three times weekly?

Do you have a creative hobby (gardening, painting, needlework etc.)?

Do you take part in any non-competitive sport (walking, swimming, cycling), or belong to a yoga or exercise class?

(✓) (±) (✗)

Do you try to have a siesta or short rest
  period during the day?
Do you have regular massage or
  osteopathic attention?
Do you spend at least half an hour
  outdoors in daylight each day?

The first six answers should be 'no'; all 'yes' answers here
show a need for modification. The answers to the next six
questions should be 'yes'; all 'no' answers show a need for
modification.

More on Time Management

The answers to the following questions should be 'no', and
any 'yes' answers will guide you to action which is
explained in later chapters.

Do you commonly find yourself doing more than one
  thing at a time?
Do you usually try to finish any given task as fast as
  possible?
Do you seldom plan in advance how you will use your
  day for things which need doing?
Do you find yourself getting very impatient and angry
  if things don't go smoothly?
Do friends and family tell you that you work too hard?
Do you commonly feel 'wound up', supercharged,
  unable to stop?
Is there seemingly never enough time for hobbies?
Do you have the feeling when travelling anywhere that
  the journey itself is a waste of time?

Environmental Factors and You

1. Do you live in a noisy neighbourhood?
   (If 'yes', deal with the cause if possible, or wear earplugs at night, and practise relaxation)
2. Do you live in a polluted neighbourhood?
   (If 'yes', take antioxidant nutrients, such as vitamins A, C and E, and consider moving)
3. Do you get physically stiff, achy, because you sit for too long, or work in uncomfortable positions?
   (Pay attention to the furniture you use, and how you sit and stand in your work and leisure. Ergonomically designed furniture is available; do regular yoga-type stretching exercises, have regular bodywork – massage, osteopathy etc.)
4. Do you become increasingly depressed in the winter?
   (You may be suffering from seasonal affective disorder (SAD) and need more time exposed to outdoor light, or to obtain full-spectrum light for your home/workplace)
5. Do you find your home constricting, lacking in space or privacy?
   (Pay attention to optimal use of what space there is by use of storage units, screens etc., and to avoiding undue clutter and untidiness; ensure private space and time)

Learning to Respect Your Body Signals

Your body is a remarkable self-balancing organism. It has multiple systems of checks and balances, and it provides clear signals to its needs. Do you ignore them?

1. Do you commonly over-ride feelings of tiredness by pushing yourself to carry on, or by using stimulants (coffee, sugar-rich food, alcohol, tobacco etc.) to provide a 'boost'?
2. Do you ignore the urge to go to the toilet, with thoughts of 'I haven't got time for that'?

3. Do you skip meals by having snacks, or stimulants, as in question 1, or by just ignoring hunger?
4. If you feel a yawn coming on do you try to suppress it?
5. Do you consciously sleep for less time than you know you need?
6. Do you commonly work through your lunch period unaware that you should have a break, if not for food, then for a rest, a walk or a nap?
7. Do you commonly ignore feelings of thirst?
8. If you feel aches or pains, do you ignore them as being unimportant, or a nuisance?
9. Do you feel irritated with yourself/your body when you start to feel tired?
10. If you have a cold, or flu, or other minor illness, do you ignore it, take something to deal with the symptoms perhaps, and just carry on as normal?
11. If your health is enquired after by a close family member, or a friend, do you give a standard answer rather than telling the truth?
12. When you see people greeting each other with a hug, do you long for some of the tender loving care which it represents, or do you feel it's a waste of time?

Any 'yes' answers in this section indicate that you are not adequately taking account of, and respecting, the needs of your body and mind. The long-term effects of this are likely to show as chronic problems of one sort or another, both physical and emotional (and a likelihood of fatigue, insomnia, frequent infection, allergy, constipation, aches and pains etc. developing).

Your immune (defence) system is certainly unlikely to thank you for ignoring its needs, and it might not respond efficiently when you most need it to. You would be well advised to start listening to your body's signals, and responding to its needs.

The suggestions for change made in the next chapter are designed to modify negative habits and behaviour patterns, as well as improving the entire functional ability of the body to cope with stress. As has been indicated in earlier chapters, some such changes require a firm attempt to alter entrenched attitudes. The checklists will have shown some of the ways in which you need to act to reach the desired aim, i.e. nutritional reform and increased attention to exercise. The more comprehensively these ideas are pursued, the quicker and more dramatic will be the improvement in health, ability to function and, in consequence, stress reduction.

In subsequent chapters, methods of relaxation and meditation will be presented, which, when added to the other modifications, will indeed revolutionize the mind and body. Positive health is rare today, and this is the ultimate aim of us all, since, through a healthy body, we have the opportunity to achieve the ultimate human desire, which is to be happy.

How would you recognize stress-free good health? One set of characteristics could include: sleeping soundly; waking refreshed; having a good appetite and boundless energy; having no obvious health problems, or pains; being clear-minded and able to concentrate; enjoying life, with an optimistic attitude towards the future. Most people, I believe, would settle for that sort of state – it is certainly worth making an effort to achieve it.

CHAPTER 6

Starting to Stress-Proof Yourself

All of those aspects of your life which are within reasonable control should be examined and, where desirable, adjusted to (a) minimize stress, and (b) raise the level of health and well-being. In this chapter I examine the following factors with those two aims in view:

1. Diet and nutrition
2. Exercise
3. Breathing
4. Sleep
5. Environmental factors
6. Lifestyle
7. Attitudes and beliefs
8. The role of psychotherapy

1. Diet and Nutrition

A well nourished body will function more efficiently than one which is not. A well nourished body will stand up to stress more successfully than one which is not. The majority of people in industrialized countries are not well nourished. Indeed, evidence is growing that, in all social classes, the majority of people are deficient in one or more nutritional elements. A number of surveys conducted in the UK and the USA show clearly that the so-called 'balanced diet', which is supposed to provide all the essential elements of life (protein, minerals, vitamins etc.) is largely a myth.

In 1980 the Bateman Organization conducted an in-depth survey into people's eating habits in the UK. The results showed that only 15 per cent of those interviewed were consuming a diet which could provide even the minimum requirements, as recommended by the Health and Social Security Service. In the USA Drs Ringsdorf and Cheraskin have detailed a survey of 860 patients at the Alabama School of Dentistry which showed that around half had possible vitamin C deficiency states, and 6.6 per cent had no vitamin C in the blood at all. A further survey of 120 randomly selected patients at Jersey City Medical Centre showed 88 per cent had a significant deficiency of at least one vitamin, and 63 per cent were deficient in two or more vitamins. Dr Geoffrey Taylor, in an article in the prestigious *Times Health Supplement* in January 1982, stated that '20 per cent of elderly out-patients, 46 per cent of patients with severe chronic disease and 50 per cent of institutionalized elderly people were shown to have levels of vitamin C at which scurvy occurs.'

Amongst the general public, there is an assumption that a normal balanced diet will provide all that the body needs to maintain health. Even if there is some nutritional knowledge (and this is true in only a minority of cases), modern agricultural and commercial practices work against the diet actually containing the nutritional level which it is supposed to. Loss of nutrients starts in the soil, where much land is deficient in trace elements, and elements such as zinc, due to the continual heavy use of synthetic fertilizers and over-cropping. Crops are therefore similarly deficient. Further loss of vitamins and minerals occurs between the time of picking and eating, especially where any form of processing is involved. The eating pattern of civilized peoples, with the enormous increase in the consumption of refined carbohydrates and sugars, has deprived the public of complex carbohydrates with their essential nutrients.

High sugar consumption provides many calories, but no nutrients. This can lead to the condition known as hypoglycaemia (low blood sugar), which produces wild swings in mood and behaviour. Characteristic symptoms of this include irritability, fatigue and dizziness. When your blood sugar is low, you are liable to react unpredictably to external stress factors, and you are more likely to generate stress emotionally because of unreasonable feelings of edginess.

Industrialized societies create environments in which there is inevitably pollution of water and air, and consequently the absorption by the public of toxic, heavy metals, such as lead, cadmium and aluminium. All these and other factors can result in you feeling below par. Irrespective of feelings, any nutritional deficiency makes the body less resistant to stress. One essential nutrient which is frequently lacking in a 'civilized' diet is zinc. Dr Carl Pfeiffer, in his book *Zinc and Other Micronutrients*, states that a deficiency of zinc, among other things, results in behaviour changes and confusion. Under stress, more zinc than usual is excreted, with consequent aggravation of such symptoms.

In their book *Psychodietetics*, Drs E. Cheraskin and W. Ringsdorf (Bantam, 1976) quote other examples of common deficiencies in relation to stress.

Relatively few people suffer from the most easily diagnosed nutritional ailments. The majority limp through the haze that lies between the daylight of optimal health and the darkness of absolute illness, trying to cope with varying degrees of mental disability.

People don't 'go crazy' suddenly, although they may

appear to. Only bones crack from one sharp blow. Prior to an emotional breakdown, chemical imbalances have progressively worsened. The patient has grown increasingly anxious, developed additional physical and emotional symptoms so diversified that they defy a physical diagnosis, but fit nicely into psychiatry's dictionary.

About five per cent of the population suffers from what psychiatrists call anxiety neurosis. Typical symptoms include nervousness, exaggerated fears, sleep disturbances, general pervasive feelings of impending doom, and loss of appetite.

Dr John Wozny, a University of Alberta psychiatrist, has found that calcium therapy works wonders for the anxiety-ridden. One of his patients, a thirteen-year old with a long history of emotional complaints, was a bundle of nerves. Tense and friendless, tortured by morbid fears, she particularly dreaded test days at school. Other psychiatrists who treated her had attributed her symptoms to an insecure family atmosphere.

Dr Wozny tested for a nutritional disorder and recommended a high calcium diet. Twenty-three days later, the girl's fears and anxieties were overcome, she was able to get a full night's sleep, and she showed marked improvement at school.

In anxiety neurosis, as in so many other emotional ailments, vitamin deficiencies play an important part. Recent research has uncovered the fact that school children with poor appetites, slow growth rates, and a subnormal sense of taste and smell, are suffering from zinc deficiencies.

Zinc deficiency is more prevalent than supposed. Food refinement and zinc-depleted soils produce zinc-depleted plants, fruits, vegetables, grains, and animals. Dietary zinc supplements, and complete mineral or vitamin supplements containing zinc, are one answer. Foods from the sea, particularly herring, oysters, and sardines, offer plentiful supplies. Nuts and seeds are also good sources of zinc.

As with zinc, so with magnesium. Deficiencies are no longer rare. Magnesium is vital for nerve condition, muscular contraction, and the transmission of impulses all along the nervous system. Dr Willard A. Krehl of the University of Iowa, analysing a group of patients with mild magnesium deficiencies, found that 22 per cent had convulsions; 44 per cent suffered hallucinations; 78 per cent showed mental confusion; 83 per cent were disoriented . . . and 100 per cent startled easily and were alarmed by unexpected movement or noise.

These examples should help you to realize that one factor that is within your control, namely diet, can substantially improve your body's ability to cope with stress, as well as helping towards higher levels of function and well-being. The opposite is also true, of course, and by eating in an unbalanced manner, levels of well-being will be reduced, and the effects of stress are then more likely to be harmful. Poor diet could well be called the 'primary stress factor'.

Food and Mood

There is also the fact that research has shown the tremendous influence the food we eat can have on our mood, the way we feel . . . and, therefore, how it can be a major element in determining how we behave, react and even think, when exposed to life's stresses.

Take the controversial amino acid tryptophan (recently banned from sale and use due to a contaminated batch causing serious illness, despite the fact that this only happened with one manufacturer's product). Tryptophan, which is present in all dairy and animal proteins, and in many vegetable sources as well, is an 'essential' amino acid, which means it, along with seven other essential amino acids, has to be present in your diet so that your body can manufacture all the thousands of different proteins and other substances it needs to build tissues.

If you eat an abundance of foods rich in tryptophan (such foods as fish, pasta, rice, soyabeans or their products, pumpkin seeds, sesame seeds, walnuts, bananas or chicken in which it is well supplied) there will occur, in your brain, an increase of manufacture from it of the neurotransmitter serotonin, which will encourage relaxation and a sense of calm well-being (*Thorsons Guide to Amino Acids*, Leon Chaitow, Thorsons, 1991).

If you have an excess of it (hard to do from food alone, but not difficult from supplementation, when this becomes legal again) actual drowsiness can occur (as a result tryptophan has long been successfully used to treat insomnia, and this fact partially accounts for the value of a late night protein snack for people so afflicted.) Conversely, when tryptophan is very low in the diet research has shown that aggressive behaviour increases, and where violently aggressive individuals are supplemented with a high tryptophan diet their aggression diminished and their mood improved ('Behavioural Ecology', S. Levine, Bioscience Vol. 2, 1982).

Allergy ('brain allergy' some people call it) to certain foods has been shown by researcher Alexander Schauss to markedly influence the mood and behaviour of juvenile delinquent offenders (*Diet, Crime and Delinquency*, Alexander Schauss, Parker House, 1980). He has shown that once sensitizing foods or actual toxins such as heavy metals (lead, cadmium, mercury etc.) are identified and removed from the diet, or body, antisocial behaviour is often dramatically modified for the better ('Behavioural and biochemical changes induced by lithium and tryptophan', P. Broderick, *Neuropharmacology*, 1973, Vol. 6, page 119).

This theme is expanded upon in the excellent book by William Philpott MD, and Dwight Kalita Ph.D., called *Brain Allergies* (Keats, 1980).

It is well established that stimulants such as caffeine and alcohol can alter mood for better or worse, depending on the amount used and the degree of sensitivity, but it is perhaps not so widely realized that one of the most common mood altering substances is refined sugar, which is so rapidly absorbed into the bloodstream that it produces an instant 'high' in which energy is increased, tiredness vanishes (temporarily), and all things seem possible. Unfortunately, the self-regulating mechanism of the body so efficiently deals with the potentially damaging sugar rise, by pumping out substances such as insulin, that the sugar level drops, and along with it your mood and energy status. So the sugar-junkie once again boosts the levels through another 'fix' of sugar-rich foods or drink (or by using caffeine, alcohol or tobacco which boost sugar levels through stimulation of the adrenal glands.) This cycle of sugar highs and lows, often also associated with high-pressure lifestyle behaviour (too little sleep, too much activity and stimulation, either in work or play) is a recipe for health disaster if prolonged, and is a major physical and emotional stress factor, leading all too often to symptoms of tiredness, depression and irritability.

Then there is the question of whether any of these things are occurring in a setting of actual underlying nutritional deficiency, which would compound and complicate any effects on mind and mood.

Signs of Deficiency

The following symptoms are common signs of vitamin and/or mineral deficiencies (there are many others):

- Tongue and inner lips are bright red instead of a usual pink colour.
- Corners of the mouth are cracked.
- Skin scaling at edges of nose.
- Nails are ridged, brittle or soft.
- Receding gums that bleed easily on brushing.

- Changes in texture of skin, such as dryness with a tendency to crack or flake, especially on thighs and lower abdomen.
- Lifeless, thin hair with scurfy tendency.
- Swollen inner surface of lower legs and ankles.
- Bruising easily.
- Low vitality, apathetic and listless.
- Slow-healing grazes and cuts.
- White flecks in nails.
- Poor dream recall.
- Tendency to stretch marks on the skin.

The pattern of eating advocated to achieve a balanced diet is as follows: Fifty per cent or more of your diet should comprise raw foods, such as salad, fruit, seeds, nuts and cereal mixture. One of your main meals should be a salad-based meal with wholemeal bread or a jacket potato and cheese. The other main meal should contain 4-6 oz (100-150g) of protein, either animal or vegetable, and extra vegetables. Dessert should consist of fresh or dried fruit. Snacks should consist of fruit and seeds (sunflower etc.). Drinks should be taken between meals; either fresh fruit or vegetable juice, spring water, a herb tea, coffee substitute or a yeast-type drink are all suitable alternatives.

Things to Avoid Where Possible

- All white flour products, such as white bread, cakes, pasta, pastry and biscuits. Replace them with their wholemeal equivalents (available at health food stores).
- All sugar of any colour, and its products, such as sweets, jams, soft drinks, ices, etc. Replace these with fresh fruit, dried fruit, sugarless jam, fresh fruit juice, etc.
- Polished white rice. Replace this with unpolished brown rice.
- Any foods containing additives, preservatives, colouring, etc., such as most tinned foods.

- Tea, coffee and chocolate. Replace with herb teas, dandelion or other coffee substitutes.
- Strong condiments, such as vinegar, pickles, pepper, curry etc. Replace with herbs.
- Alcohol (with the exception of a little wine or real ale).
- Margarine.
- Salt and salted foods.

Supplements

The following supplements are suggested for anyone actually suffering from signs and symptoms related to nutritional deficiency or stress. Dosages are arbitrary, and could be excessive (harmlessly so) for some, but low for others, since it is known that everyone has individual needs:

Vitamin B complex	1 well-formulated tablet daily, or 8 brewer's yeast tablets
Vitamin C	1g daily
Vitamin B3	(niacin or nicotinamide) 500mg daily
Vitamin B5	(calcium pantothenate) 500mg daily
Vitamin B6	(pyridoxine) 100mg daily
Calcium and magnesium	1g calcium citrate and 500mg magnesium
Zinc	(zinc orotate or aspartate) 200mg daily
Potassium	(potassium orotate or aspartate) 150mg daily
Manganese	(manganese orotate or aspartate) 150mg daily

All should be taken with food.

To understand the reasons for these suggestions I

recommend the following books: *Psychodietetics* by Cheraskin and Ringsdorf (Bantam, 1976), *Mental and Elemental Nutrients* by Dr Carl Pfeiffer (Keats, 1975), and *Brain Allergies* by Drs William H. Philpott and Dwight K. Kalita (Keats, 1980).

2. Exercise

Regular physical exercise is essential for optimum health. The physiological processes of the body (circulation, respiration, etc.) will improve in function only if exposed to controlled exercise. Lack of this results in inevitable, slow, but progressive deterioration. In order to cope with the physical and emotional stresses of life, physical fitness is obviously an advantage. It is probably undesirable for highly stressed people to participate in competitive sport, since additional stresses frequently occur through competition itself.

Symmetrical forms of exercise, which employ all or most of the body musculature, are the most beneficial. This would include walking, running (jogging), skipping, swimming, cycling or rowing. There is a well-known physiological response to vigorous exercise. The body was designed for activity, and the old saying 'what you don't use you lose', may well be applied to muscular strength and functional ability.

In relation to stress, in particular, it has been noted that the hormone, epinephrine (adrenalin) is produced in large quantities, after only ten minutes of sustained activity. This hormone is linked with a general feeling of happiness. Also, as the circulation is rapidly stimulated by exercise, it reduces the presence of lactic acid which results from shallow breathing and inactivity. Lactic acid can induce feelings of fatigue in muscles, and is responsible for dulling the brain's activity. The effect of exercise on the system as a whole activates the hormone-producing endocrine glands, stimulates the vital organs, and has a definite, positive effect on lethargic, bored and depressed states of mind.

There is a great advantage in reducing muscular contraction and tension, which may often result from emotional stress, but which may also be caused by lack of exercise, poor posture and habitual working positions. Such muscular tension feeds back impulses, via the nervous system, and creates a degree of central nervous system activity which prevents you from relaxing mentally. In other words, just as mental states can create physical (in this case muscular) tension, so can a prolonged degree of muscular tension influence the emotional and mental state. Physical exercise (as well as relaxation techniques and deep massage or manipulation of the soft tissues) can reduce such tension in the muscles.

There is also the sense of well-being that derives from the release of muscular tension and improved circulatory and respiratory functions. Advice should be sought concerning your individual needs in terms of exercise if you have any health problems. However, as a general guide *Aerobics* by Dr Kenneth Cooper is to be recommended. This book explains the whole background to this essential part of stress reduction and health promotion.

In general terms, unless there are medical reasons why not, everyone should have twenty minutes active exercise four times a week. It is helpful to monitor your pulse rate in order to achieve the optimum effect, and not to overstrain the physiological processes. An estimate can easily be made of the optimum pulse rate that you should achieve and maintain during exercise. If you don't reach this level the exercise will have less than its maximum beneficial effect, and if you exceed this rate there may exist a risk of strain to the heart. To estimate your desirable pulse rate, use this handy formula:

From 220 deduct your age, and multiply the result by

three and divide by four. The product is your target to aim for.

For example, if you were aged 40:

$$220 - 40 = 180$$
$$180 \times \text{¾} = 135$$

A pulse rate of 135 should not be exceeded during exercise by a 40-year-old, but this level should be reached. Progressively, it will be found that more exercise will be required (in terms of effort) in order to reach this level. This shows that fitness is being achieved.

Many researchers have reported that a physically conditioned person performs tasks such as an aptitude test with better results than before undertaking such a course of physical exercise. It doesn't seem to matter whether the predisposing factors towards negative health factors are physical or psychological, a healthier response is likely to be achieved from a mind in a healthy and fit body.

The essential aspect of exercise, in a stress-reducing programme, is that it should be co-ordinated to a person's needs. This is where Dr Cooper has made such an important contribution, by producing a workable definition of physical fitness, linked to a workable way of measuring the various forms of exercise in relation to a person's age and present fitness. Here is an example of the detailed manner in which 'aerobics' graduates the degree of exercise required.

Males aged between 20-49 score a 'good' for covering 1.5 miles in 12 minutes (running). If they run 1.65 miles, this is excellent. Walking 4-5 miles at between 15-20 minutes a mile, is the equivalent of this, as is swimming 950 yards in 2.5 to 3.2 minutes per 100 yards, or cycling 9 miles at between 4 and 6 minutes per mile. Five such performances weekly are said to maintain good physical condition.

This example shows the usefulness of following Cooper's programme for a variety of exercise with which to produce tangible and desirable targets. Apart from the effects on stress and general health, such regular physical exercise has, of course, dramatic beneficial effects on heart and circulatory function, which is what it was originally designed for. Can exercise really influence stress and emotion? The following extract from *Health for the Whole Person* by Drs Hasting, Fadiman and Gordon (Westview Press) gives some indication of the possible value.

> The anecdotal evidence includes claims in books and in the popular press by varied authorities that fitness routines enable people to do more work, to feel and look better, to feel more spontaneity and joy in life, and to minimize their high risk behaviours. Psychiatrists and other mental health professionals, committed to various physical disciplines, also claim that regular participation lessens depression, improves self-image, diminishes hypochondriacal behaviours, and mitigates muscle tensions and anxieties.

Dr Kenneth Cooper claims that observations at his Aerobics Centre in Dallas, and elsewhere, support his view that physically fit people are also psychologically fit. Although he steers clear of a cause and effect explanation, Dr Robert Brown at the University of Virginia states that neither he nor his colleagues have ever treated a physically fit, depressed person.

Thaddeus Kostrubala (1977), a psychatrist and the author of *The Joy of Running* (Pocket Books, New York, 1977), goes farther than most. He claims that running can – in some cases – cure mental illness. In an article by the same title that appeared in *Runners' World* (January 1978), Kostrubala is quoted as suggesting a running regimen for patients diagnosed as schizophrenic. The article cites two studies. The first study at the University of Missouri involved 100 teachers who participated in swimming, weight-lifting, cycling and jogging. It indicated that all those who showed emotional depression in testing before the six-week programme showed an improved state of mind at the end of the experimental; period. The second study conducted with prisoners and police officers in training under the direction of Dr William P. Morgan of the University of Wisconsin yielded similar results.

Practitioners of fitness disciplines have also reported states of extreme calm or centeredness, oneness with the universe, and transcendence. This is often the case with marathon or distance runners, but it also occurs with T'ai-chi, swimming and other disciplines (Murphy and White, 1978). Until these studies are replicated with appropriate controls, we can only speculate about their implications. In any event, those mental health professionals who also pursue fitness regimens and attempt to integrate the physical disciplines in their work with patients and clients, do not hesitate to mention that Freud was a great walker and that Jung practised yoga exercises to counterbalance a preoccupation with the intellectual side of life.

Vigorous physical exercise both works off the effects of stress and helps to limit it. A daily session of 20-30 minutes following 'aerobic' guidelines, or as little as four sessions of half an hour each weekly, will transform the level of mental health and produce a sense of well-being more dramatically than words can describe.

It is also desirable to include in the stress-proofing programme, one or other of a slow, stretching-type exercise, such as yoga or T'ai-chi. Initially, the more vigorous exercises are more important. Once these are established in the daily routine, lessons in yoga or T'ai-chi should be undertaken. This will greatly enhance balance, relaxation and mind-body harmony.

3. Breathing

A person's level of tension is reflected in their pattern of breathing. When relaxed and contented, breathing is slow and rhythmic, and although not necessarily deep, it should involve some movement of the entire rib cage and movement of the diaphragm. When tense, breathing is rapid and shallow. Usually only the upper part of the chest will move, and the lower lungs remain virtually unused, with relatively little diaphragmatic movement. Many relaxation and meditation methods incorporate breathing into their programme, some as a major element, and others as only a minor or introductory element. Some understanding of the respiratory mechanism is therefore helpful.

The diaphragm is a large, dome-shaped muscle which forms the boundary between the abdominal cavity and the thoracic cavity. On breathing in, the diaphragm should contract and descend, thus producing a partial vacuum in the chest cavity which is filled by the expanding lungs as air rushes into them. During the breathing out phase, the diaphragm relaxes back, upwards, into its domed position. This encourages the expulsion of 'used' air from the lungs.

Breathing in is further augmented by the expansion of the ribs, aided by the muscle groups that control them, just as efficient exhalation is enhanced by the rib cage contracting. Chronic dysfunction and restriction of the diaphragm and the muscles associated with breathing, may result from a variety of causes including injury, bad posture and emotional stress. Poor breathing patterns are the rule rather than the exception in 'civilized' man.

The Hyperventilation Problem

Under certain conditions hyperventilation is not only normal, it is essential. When you run or exert yourself your body requires additional oxygen and the need to expel used air with its carbon dioxide content, or else you simply could not cope. However, when you hyperventilate (overbreathe) unnecessarily, when there is no physical demand for this additional oxygenation/elimination function, you place yourself in a compromised situation in which dramatic blood chemistry changes occur with quite startling results.

Very few people with symptoms of a phobic nature (agoraphobia – fear of open spaces and crowds, for example) or who are subject to extreme anxiety attacks and panic attacks, are free of the tendency to overbreathe. In fact, it is suggested by many able researchers, and clinical evidence, that many of these conditions, and many of the symptoms of chronic fatigue syndrome (ME), can be the direct result of hyperventilation.

Why should this be so? When you hyperventilate you literally exhale too much carbon dioxide, while taking in more oxygen than your body needs at the time. Carbon dioxide is an acidifying agent, and too rapid a loss of it causes alkalization of the blood (as carbonic acid is removed from the bloodstream), with dramatic neurological and other repercussions.

Within seconds of such a biochemical shift taking place, the hyperventilator starts to feel extreme weakness, edginess, fear and anxiety, plus a host of possible physical sensations, including faintness or giddiness (59%), tingling hands and limbs (36%), blurred vision (28%), trembling (10%), headache (22%), palpitations (42%), difficulty in breathing (53%), nausea (19%), and many others, most people suffering a number of such symptoms simultaneously, with 31% losing consciousness completely. (G. Perkin, 'Neurological manifestations of hyperventilation syndrome', *Journal of the Royal Society of Medicine*, August 1986).

Within a short time (minutes), if hyperventilation continues, a panic attack may begin in which anxiety translates into blind fear. It is not hard to see why anyone who experiences such horrible symptoms might start to exhibit fear of being in public places, especially if there has ever been such an episode when away from home, in a crowd, in a public place. Far better, they might feel, to suffer in the safety and privacy of their own home.

Unfortunately, such avoidance tactics (staying at home) can all too easily become habitual, and the initial fear turns into a terror as the phobic pattern becomes established. Hospital studies (St Bartholomew's and St Thomas's in London, for example) have shown that not only can agoraphobics, and others with phobic and panic attack symptoms, be helped by dealing with the hyperventilation, but so can many people with chronic fatigue.

Dr L. Lum, Consultant Chest Physician of Papworth Hospital, Cambridge, states that hyperventilation is 'pure habit'. He says: 'Excessive sighing, sniffing, nervous cough, and such habits are often family characteristics.' He points out that common amongst his hyperventilator patients are actors, singers and athletes, and that the majority of patients are people who are mildly obsessional (perfectionists) and Type A personalities who drive themselves too hard, or who set themselves goals at the very limit of their reach.

The knowledge that faulty breathing habits can cause anxiety states resulted in breathing retraining being used to treat the condition, with astounding results. Dr Lum reports that more than 1,000 patients have received breathing retraining and relaxation instruction in his physiotherapy department, and that anxiety symptoms are usually abolished within one to six months, with younger patients often requiring only a few weeks.

Only about one patient in 20 failed to respond to this approach, and it was found that 75% of patients were clear of all symptoms at 12 months follow-up, and a further 20% had only mild symptoms, having lost their anxiety ('Hyperventilation and anxiety states', *Journal of the Royal Society of Medicine*, January 1981).

A further complication is found in people with hyperventilation tendencies who talk a lot, since they tend to swallow air as they talk (this is known as aerophagia, and it happens because they do not allow enough time to swallow between sentences.) All too commonly, swallowing also becomes more frequent in such people, going up from an average of 6 to 10 swallows per hour to as much as 100 in some cases. The result is that they may swallow large amounts of air, leading to a grossly distended abdomen, belching and very often to aggravation of pre-existing hiatus hernia symptoms.

Treatment by breathing retraining, relaxation exercises, biofeedback and behaviour modification resulted in marked improvement in many cases studied (S. Calloway, 'Behavioural techniques in the management of aerophagia in patients with hiatus hernia', *Journal of Psychosomatic Research*, Vol. 27, 1983).

How Can You Know if Hyperventilation is Causing Your Symptoms?

In hospitals many doctors use a 'provocation test', which simply means they ask the patient to deliberately hyperventilate, and they watch to see whether their symptoms (anxiety, etc.) appear. This is slightly risky since the symptoms can be severe and difficult to control in rare instances. A less risky approach is used by Dr Peter Nixon of Charing Cross Hospital. He and his team have developed a 'think' test, in which they carefully observe their patients during the initial case-history taking. Any subject, or area of discussion, which appeared to disturb the breathing rhythm is carefully noted down, and later on the patient is asked to sit quietly and to think of that topic. If hyperventilation starts to develop it is not difficult for the consultant to then calm matters down and 'switch off' the impending attack. (P. Nixon et al, 'The Think test', *Journal of the Royal Society of Medicine*, May 1988).

This is not something you should try to do without supervision, so how can you obtain clues on whether or not hyperventilation is a problem in your case?

Two Simple Tests

1. Sit in front of a mirror, and when you are quite relaxed, take a fairly deep breath, observing what happens to your shoulders as you inhale. Do they rise towards your ears more than just a little? If so, you may be hyperventilating habitually (unless you are an asthmatic, in which case this would be a common pattern.)
2. Stand and place one hand on your stomach just below your rib cage, and the other on the central portion of your upper chest. Breathe slowly and deeply. Does your lower hand move first as you breathe? Or, does your upper chest hand move first? If your lower hand is the first to move, this indicates a more normal breathing pattern. If, however, your upper chest moves before the abdomen (diaphragm) it indicates an inefficient breathing pattern which would accompany hyperventilation.

What to Do if You Hyperventilate

You should get professional advice, of course, but you can do much for yourself by following the breathing and relaxation advice which follows. However, as a first-aid measure rebreathing can help calm matters.

To rebreathe, use a paper (never plastic) bag which you hold over your mouth and nose, and into which you exhale, rebreathing the 'used' air. This will push up the level of carbon dioxide intake, and neutralize the alkaline blood state. Continue doing this until all symptoms abate.

Breathing Exercises

Breathing is the one vital function over which we can exercise voluntary (i.e. conscious) control. Its intimate connection with our emotions allows us an opportunity to influence the effects of stress and tension for the better, by learning how to introduce a correct, natural, full breathing pattern at will.

The following breathing exercises are designed to help you to learn how to breathe fully, so that in stressful situations and environments you will be able to unobtrusively put one or other of them into practice, and thereby overcome the tendency to shallow, tension-induced breathing. The exercises can be practised when standing, walking or at rest. Also, they can often be helpful in inducing sleep in people with a tendency to insomnia.

Before learning the exercises, though, you should be aware of the phenomenon of 'over-breathing'. In many people under stress there exists a tendency to sigh, catch the breath, gasp and generally to introduce 'laboured' heavy breathing. In a crisis this might well be an appropriate response (see the section on the 'fight and flight' reaction in Chapter 2), but in the aftermath of a crisis it is not appropriate. Unfortunately, such people seem unable to return to a normal pattern of breathing, and continue to hyperventilate.

There is a tried and proven technique which can be used to deal with chronic over-breathing habits, and it is based on traditional yoga breathing (pranayama) methods. It is useful, in all breathing exercises, to concentrate most on the exhalation phase. If this is adequate, then the quality of the inhalation that follows will be greatly improved.

The following breathing pattern involves learning two distinct lessons:

1. To use the respiratory 'machinery' correctly.
2. To train yourself to time the cycles of breathing as in the instructions that follow.

Before tackling the timing aspect, though, you need to learn the basics of good breathing.

Three-stage Breathing

Practise this lying down on your back. If your lower back cannot comfortably touch the floor, then either bend your knees, or place a cushion under them.

Stage One
- Rest your hands on the upper part of your chest, and breathe in slowly so that this part of your chest rises slightly.
- Exhale, ensuring that all the air has been expelled from your lungs before allowing the inrush of fresh oxygenated air to again expand this part of your chest.
- Repeat this five to ten times.
- Your hands should be passive, just resting on your chest and sensing the rhythmic rising and falling of your upper chest cage.

Stage Two
- Place your hands on your lower ribs, just to each side of your breastbone (sternum), so that your fingertips almost touch on exhalation.
- As you inhale, feel your ribs expand outwards and away from your body, pushing your hands apart.
- Concentrate on the exhalation being complete so that your fingertips come back together as your ribs crowd in towards the centre of your body.
- The next inhalation again produces the sideways expansion of your rib cage as air fills your lungs.
- Repeat this five to ten times.

Stage Three
- Rest your hands on your abdomen at the level of your navel.
- Begin inhalation with your abdomen expanding outwards to allow the downward movement of your

diaphragm and the filling of the lower lobes of your lungs.

- As this happens your hands will be felt to be pushed upwards (towards the ceiling).
- Exhalation reverses this, and as your diaphragm returns to its high, domed position, your abdomen flattens and your hands return to their starting position.
- Repeat this five to ten times.

The order in which you do these exercises is not important, but after practising them for some days they should be combined into the complete breathing exercise outlined below. The exercises should be done slowly – never hurried. However, if ten cycles of each stage are performed, this would only take at most four minutes – so there must be time to do them, even in the busiest day!

When you have completed practising the above three stages, start incorporating the following timing based on traditional yoga breathing patterns. These patterns have been extensively researched in recent times with astounding results.

Anti-Anxiety Breathing Pattern
The key to this remarkable method is a slow but relatively short inhalation phase, followed by a slow *controlled* but significantly longer exhalation phase. The ideal to aim for – and this may take weeks of practice to achieve – is a two to three second inhalation, followed by a very slow *continuous* seven to eight second exhalation.

This effectively reduces the number of breaths per minute to six (10 seconds for each complete inhalation/exhalation cycle).

At first it is unlikely that you will be able to achieve anything like this, so the best way to start off is to ensure that your exhalation breath takes at least a second longer than your inhalation breath, whatever its length.

For example, as you follow the different stages of three-stage breathing, try to breathe in for two to three seconds, and out (after the slightest of pauses) for three to four seconds. Concentrate your mind on the breathing out phase, ensuring that this is fully complete before starting the next inhalation. You can actually use your own hands, as they rest in the different positions described above, to lightly compress your rib cage on exhalation to squeeze the last air out, so to speak.

Practise this sort of timing for some days in all the positions, and then slowly extend the time taken to breathe out.

It is most important that you are breathing out slowly all the time you are counting, not blowing all the air out and just holding off from inhaling until the appropriate number is reached.

Why Is This of Value?

Studies have shown that when this pattern has been learned it can prove very effective (B. Cappo, 'Utility of prolonged respiratory exhalation for reducing physiological arousal in non-threatening and threatening situations', *Journal of Psychosomatic Research*, Vol. 28, No. 4 1984, and P. Grossman, 'A controlled study of a breathing therapy for treatment of hyperventilation syndrome', *Journal of Psychosomatic Research*, Vol. 29, No. 1, 1985):

1. It reduces arousal dramatically. This means that the chances of becoming upset or anxious after doing a few minutes of this breathing reduce markedly, whatever the stress factor involved.
2. In people with phobic or panic attack tendencies, use of this pattern of breathing can 'cure' the problem or prevent attacks if used regularly.

Complete Breathing Cycle

This should accompany the performance of the three-stage breathing, once you feel happy with your ability to do the exercises as described. It can be used on its own as a means of reducing arousal or tension at any time.

Caution: After any deep-breathing exercise it is important to rest for a minute or two with your breathing in a natural, uncontrolled pattern. Then rise slowly, first to sitting, and then to standing. It is not uncommon to feel a little light-headed for a few minutes following the full performance of all the stages of breathing. Simply doing a complete breathing cycle a few times will not produce this effect, though.

- Lie on the floor as above. Place your hands where they feel most comfortable.
- Breathe out completely, and then start the complete breath by expanding your abdomen slightly (as in stage three), filling your lower lungs with air, before allowing the lateral and upward expansion of your lower ribs to enable that part of your lungs to fill as well.
- Finally, complete the inhalation by expanding your upper ribs forward to fill your upper lungs and air passages.
- This slow filling of your whole chest cavity with its maximum capacity of air should take a count of between three and four seconds, depending upon your capacity and control.
- Count silently and slowly as you inhale and exhale with this exercise. There should be no strain involved. If you feel laboured, shorten the inhalation time.
- Exhaling reverses the procedure, with your upper passages emptying first, followed by the collapse of your lower ribs towards their resting position, and finally your expanded abdomen deflates as the used air from the lower reaches of your chest is expelled.
- Visualize a bellows emptying for a picture of what should

happen. The breathing-out phase should take substantially longer than the inhalation (say five to six seconds), with no jerking or rush, just an even release of breath.

- Pause briefly with no air in your lungs (under a second) and then allow the vacuum, which the complete exhalation has caused, to be filled as the inhalation phase starts again.
- Repeat the exercise of full cycle breathing at least ten times, and then rest for a minute before getting up.

Use this exercise whenever you are confronted by a stress situation, or when you feel 'strung up' or anxious.

Note: All breathing should be through the nose.

There are times, especially when under stress of an emotional nature, when this exercise will be more difficult to perform. The whole procedure may be jerky and accompanied by sobs or sighs. This is an excellent reason for continuing. Eventually, there may be an intense desire to laugh or cry. This type of emotional release, which may accompany deep breathing, should not be suppressed. Let it happen, and if possible pay attention to any thoughts or memories that come into your mind when it happens. These can help to give insights into underlying causes of anxiety. If it happens repeatedly, talk to your doctor about it, as counselling or psychotherapy might be a help in resolving the problem.

4. Sleep

One of the most striking symptoms of a stress condition is its disturbance of the normal sleep pattern. This may take the form of great difficulty in getting to sleep, or of waking after an hour or two of sleep and being unable to go off again, or waking after five or six hours, feeling unrefreshed, and unable to sleep again, or of the sleep itself being fitful and broken with a consequent feeling of sluggishness in the morning.

The disturbed sleep itself often becomes a source of further stress, as the person worries about not getting enough sleep, and as the effects of insomnia begin to become apparent. Sleep deprivation leads to a deterioration in perception; slower, more erratic reaction times; impairment of general performance; lower energy levels; memory lapses; increased sensitivity to pain; deterioration of judgement and motivation; impairment of concentration and a tendency towards a negative, irritable and depressed state. In mild cases of insomnia such changes may be of a slight nature, but nevertheless add to the overall stress level.

Sleep itself should be as natural and simple a part of living as breathing. It is certainly vital to health, and probably to life itself. The quality of life and the capacity to work well and to enjoy life depend upon adequate sleep. The natural rhythms of life that govern our functions are inborn. The cycles of increasing and decreasing activity are continuous within the body system. Sleep is one such cycle.

The normal sleep pattern starts with lying down, with your eyes closed, in a state somewhere between being awake and truly asleep. At this point, your brainwave pattern is called the 'alpha' state. This is the same as the state achieved in deep relaxation or meditation. Dreaming is also possible at this stage.

The next stage lasts for between 90 minutes and two hours, and takes the form of a very deep, non-dreaming sleep, known as the non-REM (REM stands for rapid eye movement) or 'delta' stage is reached. If wakened during this stage, almost nothing of what happened will be recalled, and behaviour will be zombie-like. After this, a gradual change takes place and the REM stage is reached. Dreaming begins, and the closed eyes can be seen to be moving rapidly – with body movement often occurring as well.

The significance of dreams as a source of psychological release deserves emphasis. A leading researcher, Dr André Tridon, has stated: 'The real mission of dreams is to free your unconscious, to relieve the tension due to repression and to give absolutely free play to the organic activities which build up.' Most dreaming takes place during the REM stage, which is that part of sleep most disrupted by sleeping tablets. Dreaming is felt to be important in the consolidation into memory of new information. Distressing symptoms are seen to result from dreams being constantly disturbed experimentally. Dreams are known to be vital to mental health, but whether any meaning can be divined from remembered dreams is a much debated point.

From this point on (after the dreaming stage), sleep becomes progressively lighter. It is now known that vital hormone production from the pituitary gland occurs during the 'delta' stage, and that this has a restorative and refreshing effect on the body as a whole. In civilized society, natural sleep rhythms are not given much chance to operate. There are a variety of factors which work against the sort of pattern of sleep that nature demands.

There is, for instance, a great deal of pressure in modern society towards conformity. Getting up and getting to a place of work or study, or getting up and doing what has to be done in terms of housework, family duties, shopping, etc., all necessitate waking and rising at a time that is determined, not by the needs of the body, but by whatever demands these activities make. In most industrialized societies, programmes of work or study make no allowance for rest periods during the day, and the result is, all too often, that the individual reaches the end of the working day in an overtired state. If additional stress factors are also part of this picture (difficult journeys to and from work, difficult relationships, financial anxieties etc.), then the pattern begins to look ominous.

With a combination of the above taking effect, a variety of changes can occur which are reflected in sleep disturbance. At this stage, many turn to medication for help. The results are less than satisfactory. The quality of sleep achieved by the use of sleeping tablets is poor. The drugs themselves are often addictive, and usually have side-effects, and above all else they deal (and not too well) with the symptoms and ignore the causes of illness, which is bad medicine, indeed.

Research has shown that sleeping tablets are largely ineffective, and that among the common side-effects of these drugs are indigestion, respiratory ailments, loss of appetite, skin rashes, increased blood pressure, kidney and liver dysfunction, lowered resistance to infection, mental confusion and memory lapses, circulatory problems, etc. Apart from these side-effects, most of the drugs are addictive, despite the fact that almost all sleeping tablets lose their effectiveness within a few weeks. The fact is that when they do work, they do not induce sleep, but simply knock the person out, and being unconscious is not the same as sleeping.

The greatest irony of all is that, because of their effect on the body, sleeping tablets actually result in worse insomnia after withdrawal. If sleep has become disturbed, then it is well worth considering some of the factors that can contribute towards the normalization of this vital function. From our earliest years, we establish patterns of activities that are performed before going to bed. The type of clothing worn, the type of bedclothes used, are part of the pattern. Any variation in the pre-sleep ritual can disturb sleep, and it pays to look at the sort of things that were part of the pre-sleep pattern before sleep became a problem.

Such things as bathing, putting clothes away, reading, listening to music, praying, the position of the body, and sex, among other things, all play a major part in many people's pre-sleep rituals.

If sleep is disturbed, it is often possible to compensate for it by taking a midday nap, either after or instead of a meal. This will not detract from the chance of sleeping well that night, but, by helping to restore a degree of relaxation, will actually enhance it. It is also important to ensure that adequate exercise is being taken, but not just prior to going to bed, unless this is part of the pre-sleep ritual.

Sex, or lack of it, is a major area of stress, and advice from an expert may be necessary if this is the problem causing insomnia. Individual counselling is the ideal, and your doctor should be consulted to arrange for this, if needed.

Obvious causes of a change in your sleeping pattern should be identified, and the usual routine of preparation for sleep maintained in the confidence that normal sleep will re-establish itself. There is no cause for panic or anxiety over such changes. If the change is to waking in the early hours, it often helps to get up rather than lie and worry. A great contribution towards a return to normal sleep will be made by relaxation and/or meditation exercises (see Chapters 7, 8 and 9).

Nutrition also plays a part in normalizing disturbed sleep, just as it does in most health problems. A great number of insomniacs have been found to be hypoglycaemic (sufferers of low blood sugar). This is frequently the result of a diet containing too much sugary, starchy food and caffeine-rich drinks such as coffee, tea, cola drinks and chocolate (see pages 91, 125 and 127), as well as an inadequate quantity of fresh fruit and vegetables. Many researchers have found insomniacs to have low levels of vitamin B3, B6, B12, zinc, calcium, magnesium and manganese, all of which indicates an inadequate diet. The general advice in such cases is to consult a physician who is nutritionally aware. In the meantime, follow the guidelines in the section on nutrition (page 93).

A few years ago a breakthrough in research indicated that a substance known as tryptophan plays a vital role in normal sleep. It is an amino acid, and is contained in milk, meat, fish eggs, nuts, soyabeans and other protein-rich foods. Taking concentrated tablets of tryptophan was shown to frequently hasten and prolong sleep in insomniacs, without any side-effects. This amino acid helps to produce a substance in the body known as serotonin, which appears to be vital to sleep. Your diet should, of course, supply this amino acid, but for the sleep disturbed person a 1g dose taken 20 minutes before going to bed was recommended by a major researcher in the field, Dr E. Hartman of Boston State Hospital.

Until recently tryptophan was available at all health food stores and many pharmacies, and its other useful qualities (over and above acting as a relaxant/sleep inducer) made it a phenomenally popular supplement (it was also found to help in many cases of depression, as an appetite modifier and reducer of perceived pain.)

In 1989 a number of reports emerged in America of a serious illness called eosinophilia myalgia (EM) which was reaching epidemic proportions and seemed to result from taking certain brands of tryptophan. This condition is characterized by a variety of unpleasant symptoms involving the muscles of the body, and in some instances it even led to death.

This sudden emergence of toxicity from tryptophan seemed extraordinary to those many practitioners who had been prescribing it for years with no side-effects at all, and the search for the cause led to the conclusion that a contaminant was most likely to blame at a single Japanese manufacturing plant (the American supplement industry had been importing most of its tryptophan needs from Japan). Once the tryptophan connection had been discovered, the health authorities in the US and in the UK were obliged to put an immediate ban on the further sale of tryptophan supplements, and despite the subsequent tracing of a contamination source, the ban has not been lifted.

Until the reappearance of the supplement on store shelves, the best tactic is to use foods as a means of increasing tryptophan intake. Choose from the list below and eat an hour or so before bedtime.

Tryptophan-Rich Foods

Cottage and other cheese
Skimmed and other milk
Yogurt
Eggs
Fish
Seafood
Meat
Poultry
Almonds
Brazil nuts
Peanuts
Pumpkin seed
Sunflower seed
Sesame seed
Walnuts
Lima and other dried beans
Chickpeas (garbanzo beans)

The old idea of a glass of milk before bedtime to promote sound sleep makes more sense when you know that in every gram of milk consumed there is 15mg of tryptophan. So a tumbler of milk provides just about a prescription dose of tryptophan (so does an ounce or two of sesame, sunflower or pumpkin seeds, and nuts, or an egg, or a bowl of yogurt).

Sleep is vital and sleep is natural. If it is disturbed, the causes can usually be found in the pattern of life and, by correcting this, it should return to normal. This means eating correctly, ensuring adequate exercise, practising relaxation and/or meditation, sorting out areas of stress (work, relationships, sex, etc.), and letting nature do the rest.

5. Environmental factors

Ions

Ions are electrically charged molecules present in the atmosphere around us. Some are positively charged, and others negatively. We inhale these ions as we breathe and, to a lesser extent, absorb them through the skin. In fresh air, there are between 1,000 and 2,000 ions per cubic centimetre, but in cities there are frequently fewer than 100 ions per cubic centimetre.

Ions are adversely affected by atmospheric pollution, dust, smoke, etc. They can be trapped by man-made fibres, air-conditioning, heating units and television screens. It is the negative ions which are mainly affected in this way, and it is in areas of relatively high negative ion concentration that people feel better (i.e. at the seaside or in the mountains.) Conversely, people tend to feel lethargic and depressed when they are in an atmosphere heavily charged with positive ions. This would be the case in a centrally heated or smoky room, or just before a thunderstorm or during certain seasonal winds such as France's mistral.

People react differently to ion imbalance. For some, there appears to be only a minor awareness of such variations, but for other more susceptible people a decrease in negative ionization can result in marked physiological and psychological changes. For example, there may be an increase in the production by the body of such hormones as histamine. This can result in greater tendencies to allergic reactions, as well as sleep-pattern disturbances, headaches and mood changes. Also, as a result of ion imbalance, there may be a prolonged release of adrenaline, which can produce any or all of the symptoms associated with stress (see Chapters 5 and 6).

It is now possible to restore ion balance by the use of ionizer machines. These relatively inexpensive machines can be a boon in the home or workplace to anyone suffering from these effects of the twentieth century.

Full Spectrum Light

Just as an imbalanced diet may be called malnutrition, so exposure to 'improper' light may result in an adverse health response and may be called 'malillumination'. Light is composed of waves of radiant energy and is measured in wavelengths (the distance between one wave crest and another). Sunlight produces 'white' light, which contains all the wavelengths. As well as all the colours, this also contains infra-red (heat) waves and ultra-violet (UV) waves. The full electromagnetic spectrum of waves is therefore present in sunlight.

Artificial light contains practically no ultra-violet waves and ultra-violet light is also blocked by glass windows, spectacles and motor car windshields. The spectrum of light reaching our bodies and eyes is further distorted by skin and suntan lotions, contact lenses, tinted glasses etc.

Atmospheric pollution further interferes with the full light spectrum being available to the individual. Research into the consequences of light starvation has shown that it results in potentially dramatic effects on the mind and body. The endocrine system, which produces the hormones of the body, is influenced by light received by photo-receptor cells in the retina of the eye. Acting as transducers, these cells convert light energy into chemical energy and, via neurochemical pathways, this influences the master glands in the brain, the pineal and pituitary and, through these, the whole body. There are a number of physical and behavioural effects, which have been researched in the USA by scientists such as Dr Joseph Meites of the University of Michigan, and Dr John Ott, who has written widely on the subject. He writes as follows:

'The behavioural effects of light were evident in a 1973 study of school children which we undertook in Sarasota, Florida. My experiences with trying to mature plants under fluorescent lights left me with serious misgivings concerning their extreme wavelength distortion and radiation emissions, and the possible effects of this abnormal light 'diet' on human beings. My investigations led to the development of full-spectrum fluorescent lighting, which closely duplicates the natural sunlight outdoors.

'The 1973 study, conducted by the Environmental Health and Light Research Institute, involved four first-grade classrooms. Standard, cool, white fluorescent tubes and fixtures with solid plastic diffusers remained in two of the rooms, full-spectrum fluorescent tubes were installed with lead foil shields to eliminate radiation from the cathodes. A combination aluminium "egg crate" and wire grid screens replaced the conventional plastic diffusers. In addition to allowing the full-spectrum light to pass through unfiltered, the screens grounded the radio frequency (RF) energy normally given off by all fluorescent tubes. This RF energy is known to cause inaccurate readings from computers and from the sensitive equipment in hospital scanning rooms. A Russian study reports that RF energy from fluorescent tubes has been recorded in electroencephalogram readings of human brain waves.

'Time-lapse cameras, concealed in specially built compartments, took random sequences of pictures in the classrooms. The teachers knew of the programme, but not when pictures would be taken; the children were not aware they were being photographed.

'Under the standard, cold, white fluorescent lighting, some first-graders demonstrated nervous fatigue, irritability, lapses of attention and hyperactive behaviour. They could be observed fidgeting, leaping from their seats, flailing their arms and paying little attention to their teachers.

'In the rooms which received full-spectrum lighting, the children's behaviour began to improve markedly within one month after the new lights were installed. Nervousness and excessive activity diminished, and teachers reported improved classroom performance. Many factors undoubtedly contribute to hyperactivity and learning disabilities, but these observations clearly indicate that light and radiation may be influential.

'Study of the behavioural effects of artificial illumination is continuing with animal studies at the National Institute for Environmental Health Sciences in Triangle Park, North Carolina, and with a study I am undertaking for the State of Washington penal system, to assess the effects of lighting and colours on prisoner behaviour.

'The Sarasota school experiment also included dental examinations of participating children. Those in the rooms with full-spectrum lights showed a significantly lower incidence of cavities, than those in the rooms with standard lights. Often studies with rats and hamsters suggest that the orange, red and infra-red portions of the spectrum (in which the standard, cool, white fluorescent lights are deficient) may influence resistance to caries. I suspect that some body chemicals – possibly hormones – which enhance resistance to caries, may be activated by exposure to these portions of the spectrum.'

As yet we do not fully understand the role played by light on the body. However, the examples quoted above by John

Ott indicate clearly that general health and behaviour can be dramatically influenced by attention to this aspect of 'nutrition'.

Full-spectrum lighting is available in the UK and the USA. It is also advisable to spend at least half an hour outdoors each day with your eyes unshielded by glasses. If this is not possible, being by an open window during daylight will help. Looking at the sun is not to be recommended. Full-spectrum light reaches the retina, even on a cloudy day, as long as its way is not blocked by glass. Just as proper nutrition aids stress-proofing, so does full-spectrum light, and so does a balanced ion environment.

Colour

Research is being actively conducted into the effects on mood and health of the colours to which we are exposed. Tests (such as the Luscher system), using colour cards, can assess the state of mental harmony and the general stress level. Colour is our visual interpretation of a particular band of electromagnetic radiation. When considering how colour can actually affect us, we are, to a large extent, in the realms of speculation. One theory suggests that colour acts on the pineal gland, and the pineal gland certainly does react to changes in illumination. Another theory has it that colour effects chemical changes in human cells by triggering the release of vital substances in the nerve endings.

It is now known that axonal transport is a reality and the potential of this finding is enormous. Axonal transport means that nerves do not just relay messages, but actually transport substances (protein, fats, hormones) to the areas they supply, and carry substances back towards the higher centres from these areas. If colour can affect nerve endings and alter the feedback along the nerve, then physiological and psychological change could result from this influence.

Other theories are concerned with areas not amenable to scientific investigation at this stage, such as the effect of light on the 'etheric body' or 'aura' of the individual. Kirlian photography has shown that there exists an electro-magnetic field around all life forms. Those that claim to see the aura say that its colour varies with the individual's state of health. In practical terms, blue is the colour which induces relaxation and, if possible, this should be used in clothing and decoration in preference to reds and yellows, which are stimulating and tension-inducing.

Reference to the visualization of colour will be found in the section on meditation.

6. Lifestyle – the common props

The population of the industrialized world is becoming increasingly dependent upon readily available drugs as aids to 'coping' with modern life. These range from the prescribed tranquillizing drugs and alcohol, tobacco and stimulants such as caffeine, to the use of cannabis, cocaine and heroin. The prescribed use of mood-altering drugs, such as librium and valium continues to escalate enormously. Six out of ten of all prescriptions in the USA are for one or other of these. They are considered mild, and have anti-anxiety effects. In short-term use, such as the shock experienced after the death of a close relative, these might serve a useful purpose. Long-term use, however, should never be necessary if sufficient attention is paid to the causes of the anxiety.

Librium and valium produce effects such as drowsiness, lethargy, unsteady walking, blurred vision, slurred speech, nausea, menstrual irregularity, liver dysfunction, etc. These are, however, much safer than earlier sedatives such as phenobarbitone, which blocked nerve transmission. Other sedatives had similar side-effects, as well as often producing severe liver problems and anaemia. All these drugs can produce psychological dependency if used for an extended period.

In both industrialized and under-developed societies there is a remarkable similarity in the effects upon the body in general, and the nervous system in particular, of what is eaten, drunk and smoked. Tobacco is smoked in a variety of ways, and also chewed. Alcohol, derived from an enormous variety of sources, is drunk for its rapid intoxicating qualities. A number of non-alcoholic, but equally effective drinks – such as tea, coffee, cocoa and colas – are consumed for their stimulating effects on the nervous system. The hazards of cigarettes and inhaling tobacco smoke are so well documented as to need no reiteration. The rise in alcohol consumption and the increase in diseases relating to its consumption are equally well established.

A further common prop is the use of sugar-rich foods to provide a quick 'lift'. Whether rapidly absorbed sugary foods are eaten in order to raise the blood sugar level, or whether tea, coffee, cola, cocoa or tobacco are used to stimulate the production of adrenalin, along with the release of sugar by the liver, the effect is much the same. The tired, edgy person's system is kicked back into life, much as a whip is used on a tired horse.

This repeated elevation of the blood sugar level forces the pancreas to constantly neutralize the excess sugar in the blood by producing insulin. It is worth recalling that the blood sugar level will also be increased every time there is a stress-induced reaction, as described in Chapter 5. This sort of fluctuation in the blood sugar level, combined with the strain placed on the adrenal glands and the pancreas, can result in one of several conditions becoming apparent.

Should the pancreas fail to respond adequately to the demands made of it, a diabetic state will exist. The blood sugar will be high, and the body will become unable to deal with it. There is evidence, however, that the opposite situation occurs more frequently. This involves an over-production of insulin, which leads to low blood sugar, known as hypoglycaemia. In such cases, the 'prop' has become a burden, and far from helping the stressed person, it will have added to their problems. This constant swing from a stress-induced 'high', resulting in the over-production of insulin and the consequent 'low', leads, in turn, to a quick lift being sought (through sugar, a stimulant drink or a cigarette), and thus a repeat of the cycle.

Xanthines

Coffee contains caffeine; tea contains caffeine, theophylline and tannin; cola contains caffeine; cocoa (and therefore chocolate) contains caffeine, theobromine and tannin. These substances – caffeine, theophylline and theobromine – are drugs, usually referred to as xanthines, which stimulate the nervous system, make the kidneys produce more urine, and stimulate the heart muscles and the circulation. The immediate effect after intake is a reduction in any feelings of tiredness, and an enhancement in muscular potential. Tea contains 50-125mg of caffeine per cup; coffee contains 100-150mg per cup; cocoa about 50mg, and the average cola drink contains 40-55mg of caffeine.

Reactions to caffeine vary with each individual, but if the daily intake exceeds 1,000mg (say 8-10 cups of strong tea and/or coffee and the odd piece of chocolate or cola drink), the following common side-effects are likely to be experienced: difficulty in sleeping; excitability and restlessness; trembling; palpitations; rapid breathing; ringing in the ears; acid stomach and indigestion; frequency of passing water.

Drinking the occasional cup of any of these drinks is unlikely to do any harm, but it should be noted that psychological dependence on caffeine is common, as shown by the number of people who do consume such liberal amounts of these socially permitted drugs. There are three distinct signs of addiction which are displayed by consumers of caffeine (or alcohol or tobacco) in any quantity. These are: tolerance of the drug, withdrawal symptoms and craving following deprivation. Many scientific studies confirm that all these substances do have these addictive properties.

Since society is unlikely to rapidly change for the better, it means that there is a clear choice. People must be taught to cope with stress naturally, or the use of addictive props, be they freely available or on prescription only, will continue to rise. (There may, admittedly, be times of crisis when drugs, prescribed and used with care, may be useful.) The person who knowingly relies on such drugs will also be prepared to accept the consequences in terms of diminished health levels. The person who does so in ignorance deserves pity, as well as education about the alternatives. Along with an overall reassessment of the person's diet, and the application of positive stress-reducing methods, such as meditation and relaxation exercises, the overcoming of dependence upon the common stimulant and sedative drugs will be a major step towards recovery of full health potential. It is suggested that professional help be sought if any difficulty is experienced in modifying such habits. In general, the following guidelines may be of assistance:

● *Cigarettes*: If a person smokes for stimulation, then regular exercise can help to reduce this need. If the motivation is one of enjoying the ritual of smoking, then alternatives can be found to keep the hands busy. If the smoker feels the motive is relaxation, or if smoking is a response to anger or anxiety, then the application of the techniques in this book will help to find a safer alternative. If smoking is pure habit, then a little serious thought about the consequences should aid a determined effort to stop. If there is true addiction, then very strong motivation will be needed to break the habit. Hypnotism and acupuncture can help in this, and in reducing withdrawal symptoms. Also, the taking of a number of food supplements will help. Such supplements as: a good vitamin B-complex tablet daily, 100-500mg vitamin B3 daily, 1g of vitamin C daily, and supplemental calcium and magnesium on a daily basis. Take all these with food.

● *Alcohol*: At an extremely moderate level, consumption of alcohol has been shown to have a stress-reducing effect. This level is bound to vary with individual characteristics, but it is unlikely to exceed the equivalent of 1½ glasses of wine, ¾ pint of beer, and one measure of spirits, daily. Anything in excess of this is almost certain to create more problems than it solves. If difficulty is experienced in keeping consumption to this level, then it may be better to stop altogether.

A number of nutritional aids exist to assist with the withdrawal symptoms experienced by regular consumers of alcohol when they stop or cut down their intake drastically. One of these is an amino acid called L-glutamine. It is suggested that three 500mg tablets be taken daily during the withdrawal stage, together with a high-dosage vitamin B-complex tablet. In addition, at least 1g of vitamin C and a multi-mineral compound should be taken. It is most important to ensure a balanced, regular dietary pattern.

Changing Your Habits

1. Avoid working more than ten hours daily, and ensure that you have a least 1½ days a week free of routine work. If at all possible, an annual holiday, 'away from it all', should be arranged.

2. During each day, have at least two relaxation or meditation periods. Time should be set aside morning and evening, or just prior to a meal.

3. Perform active physical exercise for at least ten minutes daily, for 20-minute periods four times each week.

4. Balance your diet and eliminate stress-inducing foods and drinks.

5. Try to move, talk and behave in a relaxed manner.

6. Seek advice about any sexual or emotional problems that are nagging away at the back of your mind, or which are causing conscious anxiety.

7. If there are actual stress-inducing factors at work or home, which can be altered, then take definite steps to make these changes.

8. Cultivate a creative rather than a competitive hobby.

9. Try to live in the present, avoiding undue reflection on past events or anticipating possible future ones.

10. Concentrate on whatever the current task is, always finishing one thing before starting another.

11. Avoid making deadlines or 'impossible' promises that could lead to stress. Take on only what you can happily cope with.

12. Learn to express feelings openly in a non-belligerent way and, in turn, learn to listen carefully to other people.

13. Accept personal responsibility for your life and health – don't look outside yourself for causes or cures, apart from the objective guidance and practical advice available from a health professional.

14. Greet, smile at and respond towards people in the same way that you would like to be treated.

15. Introduce negative ionization into your home and office, and ensure adequate exposure to full-spectrum light.

7. Attitudes and beliefs

In the field of stress there are many factors over which we have no control. We must all experience the lifestyle changes which are an inevitable part of the process of living, such as growing up, going to school, leaving home and getting work. We are all, at some time or another, subject to sudden stressful events, such as deaths and other personal natural disasters. We are, in the main, also subject to anxiety over such imponderables as world peace, economic recession, etc. Some will cope with these situations well; others will add to this list an array of self-induced stress factors which are the direct result of (a) not dealing with problems that can be solved, and (b) self-generated stress, brought about by attitudes, beliefs and personality factors, all of which may be revised or modified.

Since the objective of this book is to help people become aware of possible ways to reduce and avoid stress, some attention must be paid to these self-generated aspects of the problem.

Uncertainty is a major cause of stress, and practical steps need to be taken to reduce this factor. For example, if there is a threat of redundancy, all alternative sources of work should be methodically explored. Retraining, or updating of skills to improve future employment opportunities should be considered. If already out of work, it is vital that a person maintains the skills and knowledge they have acquired. Mind and body should be kept active, and a positive attitude should be cultivated. The alternative is to fret and become edgy and sleepless, thus reducing the chances of gaining the desired objective due to declining personal efficiency, brought about by stress.

Similar action is possible in most cases of uncertainty. For example, an unexplained symptom can often trigger the imagination to dream up all kinds of sinister implications. Once a diagnosis is arrived at, a positive course of action can be undertaken and, although there may still be some anxiety about the outcome, the main source of uncertainty and stress is dispelled.

It is always easier to cope with something identifiable, than it is with something amorphous and intangible. We should make every practical effort to reduce uncertainty, and concentrate on those things which lie within our control. In some cases, there may be no obvious action possible. It helps to talk the whole matter through with someone sympathetic, and if no course of action is identifiable, then a positive decision to shelve the whole subject for the time being may be appropriate.

Making decisions is a source of stress for many people. There is no way of anticipating all possibilities, but basic planning, using a pen and paper to help create order, is a good first step. Start by writing down the nature of the problem, and define the choices that seem to exist. One important choice should not be overlooked; that is the positive decision to do nothing. Having defined the problem and all the reasonable alternatives, spend a little time considering unusual alternatives. (This is known as lateral thinking. Most decisions are based on linear thinking, which involves starting at a given point and working towards a desired objective, and this is the best way of dealing with everyday problems.)

Having an ideal end result in mind also helps, and this should be written down too. Usually, only a limited number of choices exists, and the relative merits and demerits of these should be written down. Finally, a compromise will probably have to be accepted, for seldom is an ideal solution possible if a decision has been creating anxiety. Once the decision is made, remember that there is always room for modification if it does not prove to be as successful as hoped.

For example, a widow, living alone and not well enough to take care of herself, has two married children living in different areas. Both want her to come to live with, or near, them. Whichever she chooses, the other will feel slighted (or so she believes). What is to be done? She could either stay where she is, or go to one or other of the children. A compromise would be to spend a time with each, or perhaps to choose an alternative companion with whom to share a home. No solution is ideal, but what is vital is to make the most desirable (or the least undesirable) choice and to see what transpires. A further move is always possible if the first choice fails. It is the initial decision that creates the stress. Once a decision is made, the relative strain and stress is much reduced.

Negative Emotions

Negative emotions, long held and often unexpressed, can eat away at a person and produce great harm. Much stress is generated because of long held resentments or grudges relating to real or imagined upsets, often years in the past. One way of releasing the tensions locked up in these 'emotional cul-de-sacs' is by means of what can be called 'forgiveness therapy'. If there is anyone of whom the very thought produces a marked degree of tension, then there is probably a suitable case for the use of such therapy. In the first place, one has to realize that whatever happened lies in the past, and that nothing can change this. Second, it should be realized that holding on to a negative emotional charge over something which is past, harms only yourself, which is hardly sensible.

Whatever the circumstances, it is always possible to wipe the slate clean, and to mentally come to terms with what has happened. If practical, this can be accompanied by expressing the forgiveness openly to the person concerned, either verbally or in writing. A common reaction to such a suggestion is: 'But I don't want to reopen contact. That relationship is over and done with.' The truth of the matter is that the relationship is very much alive as long as it continues to hold such a degree of emotional power that it makes the very idea of contact repugnant. It will only be over and done with when the emotion resulting from the possibility of such contact is one of indifference; and this will happen only when the other party has been forgiven.

Personal relationships also provide a major source of stressful encounters. The more we can come to understand why we behave as we do and why others behave as they do, the easier it becomes to defuse uncomfortable and stress-inducing relationships. This principle forms the basis of a system known as 'transactional analysis'. In his book on the subject, *I'm O.K. – You're O.K.*, Dr Thomas Harris explains that in each of us there exists three states. It is as if in each adult person there co-exists the same little person he was when he was three years old as well as a 'state' relating to his parents. Furthermore, there are 'recordings' in the brain of actual experiences of internal and external events, the most significant of which happened during the first five years of life. Dr Harris goes on to describe a third state (the first two are known as 'child' and 'parent'), which is called 'adult'. These psychological states interact and influence all decisions and relationships and it pays us to learn to recognize the 'child' and 'parent' elements in our behaviour.

Childlike thought, it is said, shows itself in doubts, fears and feelings of vulnerability, with behaviour such as crying, tantrums, giggling and shoulder shrugging. 'Parent-like' attitudes show themselves in fixed positions, scolding, warning and injunctions, with behaviour such as frowning, pointing of the index finger, looking 'horrified', folding the arms across the chest, sighing, and so on.

The 'adult' state is likened to a computer, which makes decisions after weighing the information derived from the 'child' and the 'parent' and all the data which has been gathered by a lifetime of experience. In dealing with others, it pays to try to recognize these types showing themselves. If the 'child' aspect of someone is evident, then by respecting this and talking in a soothing way (just as if dealing with a child) you will reduce the chance of creating stress; for it is not childish to show the 'child' aspect, but is simply evidence of a degree of insecurity in the particular circumstances.

If you find that you are quick to take offence, then apply the old adage of 'counting to ten' for this allows time for the 'adult' in you to assess the information and to sort out the validity, or otherwise, of the initial ('parent' or 'child') reaction. In this respect, it is always best to say nothing rather than something of which you are not sure, or which you know to be a 'child' or 'parent' reaction. Of course, everyone should be prepared to listen to criticism of themselves without reacting to the fact of criticism. Listen to what is being said, evaluate it, and then either modify your behaviour or explain the reasons for it.

This attitude will avoid stressful confrontations as well as provide insights into how other people see you. Bear in mind that a major stress factor may be seen as the difference which lies between the real world and the world as the person would wish it. Their fantasy of how things ought to be is much influenced by 'parent' and 'child' attitudes. If the 'adult' can take control of the situation and apply the understanding gained through experience, then reactions would be less aberrant and stressful.

Avoiding stressful confrontations is more than just a social need; it has real health implications. It has been shown that a tendency towards hostility is often associated with a 'cynical' mistrust of others, and frequently also has overlaid a tendency to being dependent on others for a sense of self-worth.

Studies of people suffering from cardiovascular disease have shown that a high proportion have a sense of 'not being loved'. The researchers conclude that when there is a degree of cynical mistrust of others, combined with a fear of losing the affection or respect of others, an internal conflict occurs which involves persistent suppression of anger, which negatively influences the sympathetic nervous system, affecting among other things the heart and circulatory functions. The reason for this seems to be the failure to have received 'unconditional' love, affection and encouragement from one or both parents, and that this is also a major cause of 'Type A' personality behaviour. (T. Seaman, 'Social networks and coronary disease', *Psychosomatic Medicine*, 1987, Vol. 49; H. Friedman, 'Personality, Type-A behaviour and coronary heart disease', *Journal of Personal and Social Psychology*, 1987, Vol. 33; A. Fontana et al, 'Cynical mistrust and the search of self-worth', *Journal of Psychosomatic Research*, 1989, Vol. 33.)

If you recognize any of these elements in your own make-up you should realize two important facts: (a) that you are not alone, many people feel the same, and (b) counselling can help resolve much of the inner anger and hurt, and that the relaxation and other methods described below can reduce the harm done by such deep-seated personality trends.

In modifying your lifestyle to reduce stress, it is worth examining habits other than just smoking and drinking. For example, one can get into the habit of looking serious, unsmiling and severe when, in fact, it is just as easy to look carefree and to smile. The strange fact is that our emotions will respond to the way we look, just as the opposite situation is true. A friendly word, a smile, active interest in others, tolerance and praise rather than criticism, all lead to a feedback of warmth and happiness, and can enormously reduce stress both at home and at work. What is the image you have of yourself, and does it correspond to the image others have of you? If there is a lack of harmony in your environment, then it is possible that you are projecting an unhappy, stress-inducing image. The changes in thinking and behaviour that are required, need effort, but the results are worth it.

One vital point is that we have to learn to accept that which cannot be changed. Attempts must be made to minimize the effects of inevitably stressful episodes in life by means of relaxation techniques and personal development. Since it has been estimated that 85 per cent of all symptoms represent a reaction to stress, and that much illness is, at least partly, caused by the emotions, it is obviously crucial to be able to control them to a certain extent.

One frequent reaction to suggestions that a person might do best to change their behaviour is: 'that's the way I am, I can't change.' This is plainly an evasion of that which is most desirable, i.e. a modification to a less stress-inducing mode of behaviour. Change is always possible, and the way to start is to recognize the nature of the problem. A kleptomaniac may realize that, ultimately, their behaviour will lead to arrest and disgrace. The desire to avoid this may cause a determined effort to overcome the urge to steal. The end result will be added stress and the likelihood that the urge will nevertheless overcome the fear of punishment. On the other hand, if insight could be gained as to *why* a person is a kleptomaniac, not only would the desired change begin to take place, but it would be achieved without stress. The key to painlessly changing behaviour patterns lies in *understanding the reasons for such behaviour.* To achieve these insights may well require psychotherapy in one of its many forms.

8. The Role of Psychotherapy

All disease is connected in some way with the emotional, psychic or mental make-up of a person. Treatment by psychotherapy does not follow a uniform pattern. There are a wide variety of methods, all aimed at achieving an insight on the part of the patient as to the cause of their particular health problem. Such obvious symptoms as depression, phobias, neurosis, etc. lend themselves to psychotherapy more obviously than do such conditions as colitis, arthritis, hypertension, diabetes or ulcers. Yet all these conditions can frequently be shown to contain a large psychosomatic component, i.e. the mind affecting the body.

As will be seen in the section on 'guided imagery', or visualization, the main principle works two ways. If negative emotions can have adverse effects on health, so can positive images and thoughts have beneficial effects on health and well-being. Whether the psychotherapeutic method used is a traditional, one-to-one, psycho-analytical approach, or a form of group therapy which is monitored by a trained therapist, or one of the more recent forms of 'humanistic' psychotherapy, the objectives are much the same. These are to reveal aspects of the person to him or herself and, via these insights, to enable him or her to cope more adequately with life. In the process, the various symptoms would be expected to improve or vanish or, at the very least, to not get any worse.

The success of these methods depends, to a large extent, on the attitude and co-operation of the patient, who should be prepared for insights which are not always pleasant. A programme of individual sessions with a therapist and/or group sessions may continue for many months, or even years, at intervals varying from three times a week to once a week, depending on the needs of the case. In many cases, a successful resolution can be achieved in a matter of months – much depends upon the attitude of the patient and the degree of rapport with the therapist, as well as the suitability of the particular form of psychotherapy employed.

There is no particular condition which responds to a particular form of psychotherapy. Indeed, the field is so varied that no specific advice can be given. The person should seek a positive, constructive approach to their problems in all schools of psychotherapy.

Group Therapy

Group therapies offer the opportunity for people with varied background to compare and discuss their own circumstances and to observe each other's attitudes, feelings and conditions. In a much simpler manner, the group activities of Alcoholics Anonymous and Weight Watchers are based on the same idea of mutual support and release from isolation. In psychoanalysis, a far more detailed examination is made on a one-to-one basis, of the origins of the person's problems. Insights obtained by both these methods often lead to the resolution of deep-seated emotional problems.

Encounter

'Encounter' is a system which grew out of the work of an American psychologist, Kurt Lewin, who devised ways of enhancing personal awareness and personality development through training, emphasizing contact between people. This system was developed during the fifties and sixties, and is now used in a number of ways. An encounter group with a trained leader provides the opportunity for breaking down inhibitions and learning to take personal responsibility, thus achieving greater understanding of oneself, and therefore of others.

Sensitivity Training

A system known as sensitivity training was developed in America in the late 1940s. This is also known as Training Group Therapy, made up of groups of seven to fifteen people who work together to assist in gaining insights into personality and behaviour.

Psychodrama

A variation of this is called 'psychodrama', in which participants spontaneously act out dramatic roles, in the presence of a skilled therapist, in order to gain insights into deeply hidden feelings and attitudes. The roles might be those of conflict or stress, real or imagined, from the individual's past, present or future. This was a development of a Viennese contemporary of Freud, the psychiatrist Jacob Moreno.

Primal Therapy

A method developed by the American psychotherapist Arthur Janov Ph.D. is classified as 'primal therapy'. This means that it attempts to recall or realize stresses and tensions repressed since early childhood. To this end, Janov assists his patients in regressing to their infancy. Other 'primal' methods also aim at regression to childhood or to birth experience in the womb. These systems might employ dream analysis or hypnosis. New 'primal' therapies see the release of long held stresses as a natural process, which can take place once patients are encouraged to stop holding back or repressing the free expression of their basic needs.

Gestalt Therapy

Another school of psychotherapeutic thought is that known as 'Gestalt therapy'. This evolved from the work of Dr Frederick Perls, who developed his theories in the late 1950s in America. Analysis of the individual and interpretation of their symptoms and problems are avoided. The methods employed here aim at helping the individual to recognize that many aspects of their behaviour pattern, which once served a supportive purpose, are no longer relevant and, indeed, may have become an obstacle to well-being. Attention is paid to the way the individual expresses their needs and attitudes.

Body postures and movements, voice tone, physical tensions, etc., are seen as presenting vital clues to underlying stresses. By learning the meaning of these, and learning to release them, a degree of personal growth occurs. The Gestalt therapist may employ a variety of other disciplines, notably 'bio-energetics' and 'transactional analysis'. A key aspect of Gestalt therapy is to bring the individual into the present, and to enable the moment to be enjoyed to the full. Suppressed emotions and inhibitions once again have to be released in order to achieve this.

Bio-energetics

'Bio-energetics' is a system which developed out of the original work of Wilhelm Reich MD in America. It aims to bring about the healthy integration of mind and body by releasing physical tensions which accompany all psychological or emotional problems. The methods used are complex and sometimes extremely vigorous, incorporating breathing techniques, postural restructuring and the release of long held muscular stress patterns, which vary in each individual.

Psychosynthesis

'Psychosynthesis' is a system which developed from the work of the Italian psychiatrist, Roberto Assagioli, and which aims at integrating various aspects of the personality.

Voice Dialogue Therapy

A method of accessing, and thus becoming aware of the needs of, the multiple 'sub-personalities' which make up all of us, has been developed in the US by two eminent psychologists, Hal Stone, Ph.D. and his wife Sidra Winkelman Ph.D., and is described in their books *Embracing Heaven and Earth* (Devorss, 1985), *Embracing Our Selves* (Devorss, 1985) and *Embracing Each Other* (Devorss, 1989).

They have called their method 'Voice Dialogue' since one of its main 'tools' is a method of speaking to, and hearing from, the voices of the subpersonalities (or facets of the personality) which add up to the totality of our individuality. In many of us there is a denial of some aspects of their personality, a hiding away, for protection or avoidance, of essential components of our whole self. It is felt that only by making the conscious mind aware of this situation, and by hearing from both the repressed (denied) selves (all too often the sensitive, loving, childlike parts of the self) and those which are dominant and in the ascendancy (all too often the controlling, protective, critical, cynical and aggressive facets of ourselves) can an 'organic' integration begin, followed by the healing implications this carries.

The method makes no judgements or criticisms and no advice is offered, but rather the buried unconscious layers are allowed to peel away, so that through awareness of what is being suppressed, as well as what is dominant, a more balanced involvement of the many talents and facets can take place as a matter of choice.

As previously denied 'voices' emerge and begin to operate in the personality, and as previously dominant 'voices' begin to be given less power, so do major shifts occur in behaviour, energy, feelings and mood; as well as the emergence of an overall sense of empowerment, awareness and control. It is only when the conscious mind exercises control over the sub-personalities that we can operate in a balanced manner. When we carry around suppressed and denied facets of our personality, we are creating internal stresses of major proportions, involving the potential for both physical and mental ill-health. This is doubly so if the 'protective voices' which are dominant involve aggressive, cynical and critical characteristics.

There must be times when each of us feels childish, and yet this playful 'inner child' is seldom allowed to show because 'it wouldn't look right' or 'adults don't behave like that' . . . or so says the inner critic, or the protector/controller voice which we have allowed to take over decision making of this sort.

Locked inside all of us are personalities aching to come out to play, to show their energy and light, and 'Voice Dialogue' can release them. The methods also make use of dream interpretation, since it is considered that it is through dreams that our unconscious mind reveals many hidden truths, and indeed once the 'Voice Dialogue' sessions get under way most people find their dreams becoming far more meaningful and easy to interpret. As in other systems, a 'dream diary' is kept (usually by the bed for hasty transcription of remembered fragments) and these are later discussed with the therapist/facilitator whose task it is to 'dialogue' with both the hidden and obvious 'voices' of the sub-personalities involved.

Hal Stone summarizes the aim of 'Voice Dialogue therapy' by saying: 'The course of our lives is determined, to a considerable extent, by an array of selves that live within each of us. These selves call out to us constantly – in our dreams and fantasies, in our moods and maladies, and in a multitude of unpredictable and inexplicable reactions to the world around us. The more sharply we become tuned to these inner voices, the more real choice we are able to exercise in the pursuit of our individual destinies.'

Coming into contact with our various 'selves', our denied

and our dominant 'voices', enables us to cope with stress which originates externally or internally. Fortunately Hal Stone and Sidra Winkelman have taught many therapists their methods, throughout the USA and Europe, including the UK.

Many of the ideas described above have been incorporated into humanistic psychological methodology, including variations on Voice Dialogue. Hopefully, by drawing on the valid systems mentioned above, and others of a similar nature, a synthesis of what is most useful can be found. Some methods are more suitable as a way of achieving 'growth' or 'awareness', and others are more obviously suited to releasing the stresses of the disturbed individual. All these methods have in common the over-riding interest in the patient and not the symptoms. Whether the manifestation of the psychiatric stress takes the form of physical symptoms such as high blood pressure, or psychological symptoms such as phobias, neurosis, etc., it is the underlying causes which are dealt with rather than the symptoms.

In making use of the chapters which follow, the objective should be, within a few months, to be able to give a positive answer to all, or at least most of the following questions:

1. Do you feel well?
2. Do you sleep well and wake refreshed?
3. Do you like most people?
4. Do you look forward to the future with confidence?
5. Do you enjoy life?
6. Are you normally relaxed and happy?
7. Are you regularly eating a balanced diet?
8. Do you exercise regularly?
9. Are you happy about your appearance?
10. Are you enjoying a mutually satisfactory emotional and/or sexual relationship?

The potentials for people to develop and grow as personalities are almost limitless. We have untapped resources and reserves, which most of us are never even aware of. Health and happiness are the most precious commodities on earth. The following chapters present an opportunity to acquire them.

CHAPTER 7

Relaxation Exercises

Before attempting meditation or visualization techniques (see the following chapters) it is suggested that at least one of the relaxation measures outlined in this chapter should be mastered and practised. This will greatly enhance the effect of more advanced techniques.

There are two primary areas of bodily function which are, to a degree, under conscious control, and which we can use to modify arousal, i.e. reduce stress. Recall the effects on the body of stress, in the 'fight or flight' situation (see page 20). One of the first things to happen is a tensing of the voluntary muscles, in preparation for anticipated action. At the same moment, there is an increase in the rate of breathing to meet the extra demand for oxygen made by these muscles. In attempting to relax and calm a chronic state of arousal, it is towards these two functions that attention should be directed.

It is possible to interfere with the stress cycle at other points, for example, by using biofeedback methods (see page 170); through this it is possible, amongst other things, to learn to lower your blood pressure, slow your heart rate and alter your skin temperature. Valuable as such methods are, they are simply examples of learning to control functions of the body which are normally beyond conscious control.

Critics of relaxation exercises claim that they do not fully instruct a person in awareness and correct use of their body. Systems such as the 'Alexander Technique' take many months, and often years, to teach correct use of the body and how to most efficiently and effortlessly perform any task or movement. This excellent system might well be undertaken by the person aiming for a tension-free existence as a step towards that ideal. However, it is very time-consuming, drawn out and expensive.

Whilst acknowledging that relaxation and other means of stress-proofing outlined in this book will not achieve a re-education of a person's use of their body, these relatively simple, safe and cheap methods, requiring only a little regular practice, *will* produce improvement in function, reduction of stress and greater well-being. If the person still wishes to continue to improve on this, then an Alexander teacher should be contacted.

It is also suggested that structural evaluation and, if necessary, treatment, be undertaken by a qualified osteopath to ensure that any areas of mechanical restriction, especially in the spinal and pelvic regions, are corrected prior to starting relaxation techniques.

In the initial stages it is best to practise one or other of the relaxation methods at least once, and ideally twice daily for five to fifteen minutes. Once you have tried all the methods several times each, you should be aware of which suits you best. The chosen method or methods should then be employed and practised twice daily in a quiet environment. When proficient, it will be found that this regular practice will enable you to apply the technique in any situation. Application of one of the relaxation methods when in a potentially tense or stressful situation will markedly unwind you, and reduce the physical and psychological effects which would normally become evident. Such things as stage fright, interview and exam 'nerves', frustration in a traffic jam or when late for an appointment, anger during an argument, etc., can all be reduced to a mild, controlled reaction by the introduction of such techniques.

The environment in which relaxation exercises are practised should be quiet and not unduly warm or cold. The surface on which the exercise is performed should be firm, but not so hard as to be uncomfortable, or so soft as to induce sleep. A blanket on a carpeted floor is perhaps the ideal surface.

Clothing should be loose, with no constricting or distracting elements. Remove shoes, ties, etc.; undo bras and belts. Lying on your back is the ideal position, with a small neck pillow and a bolster or cushion under the knees if your back is more comfortable that way. (Anyone who has a history of low-back strain, or who has a hollow back, will probably be more comfortable with their knees slightly flexed in this way.) Sitting in a supported position is suggested if there is any tendency to fall asleep when in the lying position.

Some adepts at yoga prefer the cross-legged, or lotus, position, and others prefer to kneel, using a small stool to support the buttocks. Whichever position is chosen, the only essential aspect as far as the first two exercises are concerned, is that you are comfortable. Later exercises will specify if a particular position is desirable. Falling asleep during the performance of any exercise is to be avoided since the aim is to practise and experience something *consciously*.

There should be no distracting sounds such as radio or TV during the relaxation period, and no sense of urgency should be felt. It is probably best not to attempt such exercises too soon after eating a meal. Morning and evening seem to be times that suit most people.

Once you have introduced your routine, endeavour not to miss practising the exercises, for it is only by persistent repetition that the first stages of relaxation will be mastered, leading on to deep relaxation and other methods of 'mind control'. At first, it may appear that nothing much is happening. Indeed, the tense person probably believes deep down that such simple measures, helpful as they may be to others, are not for them with their superactive minds which just cannot relax. Patient, persistent and thorough application will satisfy even this Type A person that the methods are indeed worthwhile.

When you begin to practise any of the exercises, you will find that intrusive thoughts come periodically into your mind to interrupt the smooth flow of the techniques. This is normal and to be expected. It should not produce any reaction of distress or anger. When a thought intrudes, push it gently to one side and resume the exercise. It does not matter how frequently such interruptions occur, simply carry on where you left off. Gradually, week by week, there will be fewer interruptions, and relaxation will deepen. Whichever exercise is being used, there should be an awareness that there is no 'correct' response. Your body and your mind will respond your way. Be passive, do not try to 'force' the exercise. Relaxation comes at its own speed. Be an observer of the processes taking place, sense changes which occur in a detached way. Let things happen and register your thoughts and feelings. Above all, be patient and passive.

1. Rhythmic Abdominal Breathing

Whilst learning the technique, arrange to have two free periods per day, each of five to fifteen minutes. Find a quiet room where you know you will not be disturbed. Rest on your back, head and shoulders slightly raised, pillow under the knees to take the strain off them and off your back. Rest your hands on your upper abdomen, close your eyes, and settle down in a comfortable position.

See that there is nothing in the way where you are lying, and nothing in the room that is going to distract your attention, such as sunlight, a clock, animals, and so on. Sitting in a reclining position is also suitable, and many people prefer this to lying down. Try both, and choose whichever is more comfortable.

Breathing is of great value in relaxation, particularly during the initial stages. People who are at ease with themselves and the world breathe slowly, deeply and rhythmically. Breathing is the only automatic function which one is capable of controlling. It is carried out partly through the autonomic nervous system and partly through the central nervous system. The autonomic nervous system is that which controls vital functions, endocrine (hormone) secretions and emotions. By controlling one's breathing, one can influence all these and, for a short time, take over conscious responsibility for them.

The aim is to breathe slowly, deeply and rhythmically. You cannot expect to do this perfectly to begin with – it might even take weeks. Inhale through your nose, slowly and deeply. Your abdomen, on which your hands are resting, should rise gently as the breathing begins. An awareness of this rising and falling of your abdomen is important to establish that your diaphragm is being used properly. Your inhalation should be slow, unforced and unhurried.

Whilst breathing in, silently and slowly, count three or four as you fill your lungs. When your inhalation is complete, pause for a second or less and slowly start to exhale through your nose, and as you do so you should feel your abdomen slowly descend. Count as you breathe out, and try to ensure that you take at least one count longer than when you breathed in (four or five). At the very least, your exhalation should take the same time as your inhalation. There should be no sense of strain as you follow the full cycle, and if you should feel that you have fully inhaled by a count of two, then so be it, for the time being. Try gradually to slow and deepen the inhalation phase, and ensure that the exhalation phase lasts at least as long. By concentrating on the exhalation phase the inhalation phase becomes easier to lengthen.

Remember to start each breath with an upward push of your abdomen. With your mind thus occupied on the mechanics of the breathing, as described above, as well as on the rhythmic counting, there is little scope for thinking about anything else. Nevertheless, initially at least, extraneous thoughts will intrude.

This pattern of breathing should be repeated fifteen to twenty times and, since each cycle should take about fifteen seconds, this exercise should occupy a total of about five minutes.

Once the mechanics and counting have become well established as a pattern, it is useful to introduce a variety of thoughts during different phases of the cycle. For example: on inhalation, try to sense a feeling of warmth and energy entering your body with the air.

On exhaling, sense a feeling of sinking and settling deeper into the supporting surface. An overall sense of warmth and heaviness accompanying the repetitive breathing cycle will effectively begin the relaxation process. Physiologically, this exercise will slow down the heart rate, reduce sympathetic nervous activity, relax tense muscles and allow a chance for the balancing, restorative, parasympathetic nervous function, to operate, as well as calming the mind.

In the initial stages this might be sufficient exercise for one session. When proficient, it can be used to precede one of the other relaxation methods and, later, in a shortened version of, say eight to ten breathing cycles, and one of the meditation or visualization techniques.

After completion of the exercise, do not get up immediately, but rest for a minute or two, allowing your mind to become aware of any sensations of stillness, warmth or heaviness. Once mastered, this exercise can be used in any tense situation with the certainty that it will defuse the normal agitated response, and should result in a far greater ability to cope.

2. Breathing and Repeated Sound Technique

Sit or lie in a comfortable position in a suitable room. Close your eyes and encourage a sense of heaviness and stillness. Focus your attention on your body, area by area, briefly, in order to assess them for obvious tension. Start with your feet and pass on to your lower legs, thighs, hips, buttocks, abdomen, lower back, chest, shoulders, neck, face, arms and hands. Do not overlook your eyes and jaw muscles. Many people screw up their eye muscles or clench their jaw habitually. If this is one of your traits, then pay particular attention to releasing these areas prior to continuing with the exercise.

This should only be a brief survey, not lasting for more than a few seconds in each region. As each area is visualized, any obvious tension should be released. If you are not sure whether a muscle or area is relaxed, tense it for a few seconds and then let it go. This brief but effective progressive muscular relaxation, area by area, prepares you for the exercise proper.

It is worth emphasizing that relaxation is a passive act. You cannot 'try' to relax, for this is a contradiction in terms. Relaxation is a letting go, a switching off, which ideally involves no effort. In suggesting that dubious areas be tensed prior to 'letting go', this is only to help to imprint on the mind the contrast between the two states. In this way, a gradual awareness will develop, enabling you to sense tension as it arises and, most importantly, to release it. (This is the basis of progressive muscular relaxation methods, and they will be described more fully in exercise No. 4.)

For the purposes of the following breathing exercise, the abbreviated method outlined above is all that is required as preparation.

● Having spent a minute or, at most, two in 'letting go' the obvious areas of tension in the musculature of the body,

begin to breathe in and out through your nose.
- Passively pay attention to your breathing and, as you breathe out, say silently and slowly to yourself any one-syllable word.
- Breathe in and out at any comfortable speed; there need be no rush, nor is there any need to make the breathing particularly slow. The rhythm should be as natural and unforced as possible, not particularly deep or unusually shallow.
- You may well find that the rhythm will alter from time to time, or that, periodically, you will let out a very deep breath, or sigh. Just let it happen, do not attempt to control the rhythm or depth of the respiration – simply use it to time the repetitive, slow enunciation of a word or sound. Many people use the word 'one' for this purpose, but any short word will do. Remember, it should be said as you breathe out. This should continue for about ten minutes.
- A feeling of stillness and calm should eventually be felt. In some cases, a sense of happiness and deep relaxation is quickly achieved. In others there is only a gradual sense of being less stressed.

In all cases, where this type of exercise is performed as described, positive physiological changes will take place, irrespective of subjective feelings. In other words, *there is a degree of stress reduction, whether or not you sense it, from the outset*. Many people expect immediate, obvious change. If disappointed in this expectation they may abandon the discipline involved in the regular performance of these exercises. This is sad and a waste, for it has been positively established that the benefits of the exercises often begin long before there is any awareness of improvement.

The repetition of the chosen word may well be interrupted periodically by intrusive thoughts. When this happens, do not feel irritated, simply resume the use of the word to coincide with exhalation. Each person will reap the benefits of this exercise at their own pace.

After about ten minutes of this exercise, stop repeating the word and simply allow your mind the luxury of doing nothing. Allow it to linger in the still, peaceful state to which you have drifted. Initially with your eyes closed, and later with them open, spend at least two minutes in this state of inactivity. Slowly get up and resume your normal activities. (It is unwise to get up too quickly after exercises 1 or 2, as over-oxygenation may result in transient giddiness.)

3. Short Alternate Nostril Breathing

There are a number of variations in applying this simple technique which has its origins in yoga. At its simplest, your right thumb is placed against your right nostril, your right index and middle fingers against your forehead, and your right ring finger against your left nostril. (Reverse all instructions if you wish to use your left hand, i.e. left thumb on left nostril, etc.)

- By pressing lightly with your thumb, close the passage of air on the right side of your nose and inhale slowly and deeply up your left nostril.
- Pause for a moment between inhalation and exhalation. During this pause, press lightly on the left side of your nose whilst releasing your thumb pressure on the right. Breathe out down the right side.
- Maintain your hand position and breathe in again through the right side.
- Again, between inhaling and exhaling, pause momentarily and reverse the pressure, so that the next exhalation is again through the left nostril. Continue as above.

Refinements of this basic technique include counting slowly to three on inhalation, pausing for a count of two, and then exhaling to a count of six. By focusing on the simple mechanics and the counting rhythm, a degree of distraction from current problems takes place.

This cycle of alternate breathing can be repeated between five and twenty times. In most cases, a sense of ease and 'letting go' takes place after about seven cycles. This exercise does not replace either of the first two exercises, but is a first-aid measure to be used any time, in any position, in addition to other methods, whenever a feeling of stress or anxiety is felt.

4. Progressive Muscular Relaxation

This method involves the systematic, conscious relaxation of all the body areas, in sequence. The position for this exercise should be reclining – either on the floor or on a recliner-type chair. Ideally, there should be no distracting sounds and the clothing worn should not constrict in any way. (A few cycles of deep breathing should precede the exercise.)

- Starting with your feet, try to sense or feel that the muscles of the area are not actively tense. Then deliberately tighten them, curling your toes under and holding the tension for five to ten seconds.
- Then tense the muscles *even more strongly*, for a further few seconds before letting all the tension go, and sensing the wonderful feeling of release.
- Try to consciously register what this feels like, especially in comparison with the tense state in which you had been holding them.
- Progress to your calf muscles, and exercise them in the same way. First, sense the state the muscles are in, then tense them, hold the position, and tense them even more before letting go. Positively register the sense of release.

In doing this to your leg muscles there is a slight danger of inducing cramp. If this occurs, then stop tensing that area immediately and move on to the next. After your calf muscles, go on to exercise your knees, then your upper leg, thigh muscles, buttocks, lower and upper back, abdomen, chest, shoulders, arms and hands, and then your neck, head and face. The precise sequence is irrelevant, as long as all these areas are 'treated' to the tensing, the extra tensing, and then the release.

Some areas need extra attention in this respect. The abdominal region is a good example. The tensing of these muscles can be achieved in either contraction (i.e. a pulling in of the muscles), or by stretching (i.e. a pushing outwards of the muscles). This variation in tensing method is applicable to many of the body's muscles. Indeed, at different times, it is a good idea to vary the pattern, and instead of, for example, contracting and tensing a muscle group, try to stretch and tense them to their limit.

This is especially useful in the muscles of the face, particularly in the mouth and eye region. Individual attention to these is important. On one occasion it would be desirable, for example, for the 'tensing' of the mouth muscles to take the form of holding your mouth open as widely as possible, with your lips tense during this phase. On a subsequent occasion, the 'tensing' could be a tight-pursed pressing together of your lips. If there is time available, both methods of tensing can be used during the same exercise, especially in the areas you know to be very tense.

The muscles controlling your jaw, eyes, mouth, tongue and neck are particularly important, as are your abdominal muscles, since much emotional tension is reflected in these regions, and release and relaxation often has profound effects.

There are between twenty and twenty-five of these areas, depending upon how you go about interpreting the guidelines given above; each should involve at least five to ten seconds of tensing and a further five to ten seconds of 'letting go' and of passively sensing that feeling. Thus, eight to ten minutes should suffice for the successful completion of this whole technique. This should be followed by several minutes of an unhurried return to a feeling of warm, relaxed tranquillity.

Focus your mind on your whole body. Try to sense it as heavy and content, free of tension or effort. This might be enhanced by a few cycles of deep breathing. Stretch out like a cat, and then resume your normal activities.

5. Autogenic-Type Exercises

True autogenic exercises need to be taught by a special teacher or practitioner, well versed in this excellent system. The modified method outlined below is loosely based on the work of the pioneer in this field, Dr H. Schultz. The distinction between a relaxation exercise and a meditation technique is blurred at all times, but never more so than in autogenic methods, which are a blend of the two.

At least fifteen, and ideally twenty, minutes should be given to the performance of this method. At another time of the day, this or another relaxation method should also be performed. This routine should become a welcome, eagerly anticipated oasis of calm and peace in the daily programme. Stress-proofing, without such periods of 'switching off', is not likely to be successfully achieved.

A reclining position should be adopted, with your eyes closed. External, distracting sounds should be minimized. The exercises involve the use of specific, verbalized messages to focus awareness on a particular area. *No effort is involved*, but simply a passive concentration on any sensations or emotions which may result from each message. Imagination or auto-suggestion has been found to have definite physiological effects. By combining a sequence of autogenic (i.e. self-generated) instructions with the passive, focused aspect of meditation techniques, a powerful method of self-help has been created.

The exercise starts with a general thought, such as 'I am relaxed and at peace with myself'. Begin to breathe deeply in and out. Feel the light movement of your diaphragm and feel calm.

Stage 1

Your mind should focus on the area of your body to which the thought is directed. Start by silently verbalizing 'my right arm is heavy'. Think of the image of your right arm. Visualize it completely relaxed, and resting on its support (floor, arm of the chair, etc.). Dissociate it from your body, and from will-power. See the limp, detached arm as being heavy, having *weight*. After a few seconds the phrase should be repeated. This should be done a number of times, before proceeding to your right leg, left leg, left arm, neck, shoulders and back. At each area, try to sense heaviness and maintain a passive feeling in the process.

Stage 2

Again, begin with your right arm, concentrating on it as you silently verbalize 'My right arm is warm'. Repeat this and pause to sense warmth in your arm or hand. Repeat this several times. The pause should be unhurried. To encourage this feeling of warmth, it may be useful to imagine that the sun's rays are shining onto the back of your hand, warming it. The sensation of warmth spreads from there to the whole arm.

Proceed through all areas of your body, pausing for some seconds at each to assess sensations which may become apparent. Such changes as occur cannot be controlled, but will happen when the mind is in a passive, receptive state. This exercise increases the peripheral flow of blood, and relaxes the muscles controlling your blood vessels. It is possible to measurably increase the temperature of an area of your body, using these simple methods.

Stage 3

This focuses on the breathing cycle with the phrase 'My breathing is calm and regular'. No conscious effort should be made to control your breathing. Unlike the form of breathing used in the exercise on page 150, this involves a passive approach. You should direct your concentration to the slight, even motion of your diaphragm.

Nothing should be consciously done about your breathing, which should be completely automatic. Sometimes the verbalized statement can be altered to 'My breathing is calm', or 'I am being breathed', to good effect.

Sometimes, quite unconsciously, a deep breath is taken during the otherwise shallow breathing. This is quite normal. Nothing should be done to control the pattern. Simply repeat the chosen phrase, and passively observe and experience the sensations that accompany it. Slow repetition of the phrase promotes deep, slow, regular breathing without effort. Continue for several minutes, repeating the phrase periodically.

Stage 4

The phrase 'My forehead is cool' is repeated for several minutes. This appears to produce a combination of alertness and relaxation. When repeating this phrase, with suitable pauses, try to sense the coolness as a pleasant sensation.

Stage 5

The phrase 'I am alert and refreshed' ends this exercise sequence. Breathe deeply, stretch, and continue the day's activities.

During stages 1 and 2, the time spent in each area should not be less than about half a minute. It is, however, quite permissible to spend two or three minutes focusing on any one part, especially if the desired sensation of heaviness or warmth is achieved.

It will probably be found that the desired sensation is more easily sensed in one stage than another, and that some areas seem more 'responsive' than others. This is normal. *It is also quite normal for there to be no subjective appreciation of any of the verbalized sensations.* Do not worry about this. Even if nothing at all is sensed for some considerable time, even some months, there is a great deal actually taking place within your body as a result of the whole exercise.

Persistence, patience and a total lack of urgency is all that is necessary for this method to lead to a decrease in muscular tension and a sense of calm and well-being. A 'side-effect' of this particular method is frequently experienced in terms of much improved peripheral circulation, i.e. an end to cold hands and feet!

CHAPTER 8

Additional Relaxation Methods

Hydrotherapy

The use of water in the treatment of a variety of conditions has evolved over the past century. Although taken for granted, water is a highly complex and vital compound. Water has a high specific heat. This means that it gives out or takes in more heat for each degree of change in its own temperature than any other substance. Water also has the ability to conduct heat more efficiently than most other liquids. A variety of forms of hydrotherapy exist, and these can be summarized as those that have a physical effect, due to pressure or mechanical stimulation (hydrokinetic), those that alter temperature (hydrothermal), and those that have a chemical effect due to the constituents of the water (hydrochemical).

Neutral Bath

There are many nerve endings on the skin surface and these deal with the reception of stimuli. More of these are cold receptors than heat receptors. If water of a different temperature to that of the skin is applied, it will either conduct heat to it or absorb heat from it. Such stimuli have an influence on the sympathetic nervous system and can affect the hormonal system. The greater the difference between the temperature of the skin and the water applied, the greater will be the potential for physiological reaction. Conversely, water that is the same temperature as the body has a marked relaxing and sedative effect on the nervous system. This is of value in states of stress, and has led to the development of the so-called 'neutral bath'.

Before the development and use of tranquillizing drugs, the most dependable and effective method of calming an agitated patient was the use of a neutral bath. The patient was placed in a tub of water, the temperature of which was maintained at between 33.5°C and 35.6°C (92°F to 96°F), often for over three hours, and sometimes for up to twenty-four hours. This is obviously not a practical proposition for the average tense person.

As a self-help measure, the neutral bath does, however, offer a means of sedating the nervous stem if used for relatively short periods. It is important to maintain the water temperature at the level indicated, and a bath thermometer should be used. The air temperature of the bathroom should be sufficiently high to avoid any sense of chilliness.

Half an hour immersed in such a bath will have a sedative or even a soporific effect. It places no strain on the heart, circulation or nervous system, and achieves muscular relaxation and a general vasodilation (relaxation and expansion of the blood vessels); all of these conditions are prerequisites of relaxation. If accompanied by breathing, meditation or visual imagery exercises (see following chapters), a fine combination of approaches towards dealing with the effects of stress will be established. This method may be used daily if necessary.

Hot Bath

A hot bath is one that utilizes water between the temperatures of 36.5°C and 40°C (98°F and 104°F). It is useful as a means of muscle relaxation, which is vital to the overall relaxation process. Five minutes immersion at this temperature is adequate to begin with. If no sensation of weakness or other untoward symptoms result, then increase the daily duration until ten minutes daily is reached. It is important to realize that a brief hot bath has quite a different effect from a long one.

Nothing is to be gained by prolonging such a bath in the hope of achieving greater benefit. Immersion in hot water acts not only on the surface nerves but also on the autonomic nervous system (that part that is normally outside our control), and on the hormone-producing glands, particularly the adrenals, which become less active. Generally speaking, a hot bath is sedative, although a long hot bath will have the opposite effect. (Some people will find the hot bath more effective than the neutral bath in achieving some degree of relaxation.)

Jacuzzi or Whirlpool Bath

This is a bath in which the temperature of the water can be controlled, in addition to there being a degree of agitation of the water by means of an electric agitator or jets of compressed air. The effect is of combined heat and massage. If the temperature is maintained at a little below 36°C (96.8°F), a relaxing effect will be achieved by ten to twenty minutes immersion.

Herbal Infusions

In all of the above-mentioned baths, additional benefit may be obtained by the use of medical or aromatic herbs in the water. Chamomile, valerian, rosemary and lime blossom, are all useful. The herb (usually 1oz/25g of the dried herb to 1 pint/½ litre of water) is boiled, and then allowed to stand for fifteen minutes. The liquid strained from this should be added to the bath. The therapeutic effects of these herbs are achieved by means of inhalation and absorption through the skin, which has been shown to be less impermeable than was previously thought.

Sauna

This Finnish method of sitting or lying in a dry, hot room for varying lengths of time appears to have a relaxing effect. In effect, though, the actual physiological benefits are minimal in terms of stress reduction. In fact, the physiological stress involved in coping with temperatures of between 75°C and 100°C (167°F and 212°F) is so profound that this system is only suitable for the very healthy.

There is some slight overall reduction in the metabolic rate after a sauna. A significant decrease in blood pressure takes place in the majority of cases after a sauna, but in 12.5 per cent of cases there is an overall increase in blood pressure. All in all, it would seem that saunas should be used only by people with a clean bill of health who are not highly stressed, and even then only in moderation. The 'relaxed' state, claimed by adherents, is probably a mild state of exhaustion.

Turkish Baths

These differ from saunas in that the degree of humidity used is far higher. The same general observations apply, though, despite this difference. These systems are fairly well tolerated by healthy individuals, but are not advisable for anyone with health problems, and it must be remembered that anyone in a stressed state has a health problem. When stressed, the response of the body can be unpredictable, and the addition of periods of intense heat can only be seen as a further stress factor.

Cold Packs

Cold packs were described by the famous nineteenth century Bavarian pastor, Sebastian Kneipp in his famous treatise, *My Water Cure*, in which he explained the advantages of hydrotherapy. A cold pack is actually a warm pack, but derives its name from the cold nature of the initial application.

The requirements are as follows:

- One piece of cotton material.
- One piece of flannel or woollen (blanket) material.
- One plastic or rubber sheet to protect the bedding.
- One hot water bottle.

The cotton material is soaked in very cold water, then wrung out well and placed on the flannel material, which is spread out on the plastic sheet. The patient lies on the damp material, which is then folded around the trunk and immediately covered by the flannel material. This is then safety-pinned firmly in place.

The top bed covers should then be drawn up over the patient, and a hot water bottle is provided. The initial cold application produces a reaction which draws fresh blood to the surface, and this warmth, being well insulated, is retained by the damp material. A 'warm pack' is produced which, gradually, over a six to eight hour period, bakes itself dry. There may be copious sweating in the process, and the material should be well washed prior to its re-use.

The pack can be slept in and should, in fact, help towards a deeper, more refreshing sleep. The overall effect is a calming one. Larger, whole body packs are also used, but they do require assistance in application, and in extricating the patient from the mummy-like wrapping which extends from the armpits to the feet. Should a sensation of damp cold be experienced when a pack is in place, it is usually a result of the material being too wet, or the insulation being inadequate or too loose.

The holistic approach to health insists that the whole person is treated, rather than just the symptoms, and that the treatment itself should not create additional problems for the patient. Hydrotherapy, when used as part of an overall attempt to remove the causes and the effects of stress, fits into the holistic approach.

Wet Sheet Pack

The wet sheet pack is the oldest and the safest naturopathic hydrotherapy method. It is safe and effective, but usually requires the assistance of someone to help wrap the sheet in place.

Method: Place one or two warm acrylic or woollen blankets lengthwise on a bed. Wring out a clean white cotton sheet in cold water and lay this onto the blankets, and lie (undressed) on the sheet so that your shoulders are just a few inches below the upper edge. Have a pillow for your head.

Raise your arms and have someone rapidly place the sheet across your body, tucking it well in the other side and moulding it to your body shape. You then lower your arms as the other edge of the sheet is brought across, covering your arms, trunk and legs, before itself being tucked under the opposite side. The blankets are then folded over so that no damp edges of sheet protrude, care being taken to enclose your feet well.

A hot water bottle can be placed at your feet, or an extra blanket provided if you feel cold for more than a few minutes.

After the first 15 minutes or so of a fairly cool to neutral temperature feeling, the sheet begins to warm up from body heat, and since insulation is efficient a period of between 30 and 60 minutes of deep relaxation ensures (this is the phase in which the sheet is around or a little above body temperature). Once perspiration starts (after an hour or so) the detoxification phase has begun, and the relaxation phase is over. At this time you should be unwrapped, rubbed down with a dry towel, and allowed to rest in a warm place for an hour or so.

The variations possible in applying this method include having the sheet more or less wrung out. The more water that is retained in it the more time and energy it takes to warm it. This requires that the degree of vitality of the person having the pack should decide how wet the sheet is to be, how cold the water is to be, how many blankets are needed, and whether a hot water bottle should be used. If the wet sheet still feels cold after five minutes, an additional water bottle should be used, and if it still fails to warm up then abandon the treatment, and use a more well wrung out sheet the next time.

Aromatherapy Bath

Before leaving hydrotherapy methods I would like to include the use of essential oils in the bath as a means of encouraging relaxation. Aromatherapy oils (essential plant oils) are now readily available from numerous sources. The water used should be just above body heat (warmer than your hand when you test it). A total of about ten drops of oil should be put into the bath as the water runs, and any one of the following mixtures of neat oils (no carrier oil) will provide a deeply relaxing experience (see *Aromatherapy* by Judith Jackson, Dorling Kindersley, 1987):

- 6 drops of lavender oil and 4 drops of geranium oil
- 7 drops of chamomile oil and 3 drops of basil oil
- 7 drops of sandalwood oil and 3 drops of marjoram oil

On getting out of the bath, rub one of the following mixtures into your skin in a slow rhythmic way:

- 6 drops of chamomile oil, and 2 drops of rose oil added to 4oz of a carrier oil
- 5 drops of lavender oil and 3 drops of neroli oil

Biofeedback

Biofeedback is a system which uses the 'feedback' to the person of biological information not usually available to them, thus enabling them to learn to exercise control over organs and functions which are normally outside their voluntary control.

By means of these techniques people have achieved control over circulatory functions, as shown by the ability to increase or decrease the temperature of a particular body area. Other examples include control of the heart rate, blood pressure, gastric secretions, brainwave patterns, skin resistance to electricity, relaxation of muscle groups, and so on. The effects of this system are profound, since such control has previously only been achieved using drug therapy.

In terms of stress and its effects, biofeedback offers a method which enables you to learn to control some of its harmful consequences. It is not certain that by learning, for example, to lower blood pressure or to raise skin resistance to electricity (both evidence of a reduction in tension), that overall relaxation is achieved. It may be that since only one physiological function is being monitored and controlled at any one time, other stress-induced symptoms might remain unaltered. A further drawback, in comparison to meditation and relaxation exercises, is that relatively expensive equipment is needed for most biofeedback monitoring. Most people, however, can achieve more rapid results by using such equipment than by using relatively slow-acting meditation and relaxation methods.

The simplest biofeedback equipment is that which measures the electrical skin resistance (ESR). Electrode pads are attached to the palm or fingers of either hand. The information derived via the electrodes is fed into a machine. This, in turn, produces a sound which is louder when the ESR is low (indicating anxiety or tension), and softer when it is high (indicating calm and relaxation). The objective is to use the mind to silence the machine. This is achieved by trial and error, until the person using it learns what to do to quieten the sound completely. At this point a relative state of relaxation will have been achieved.

A similar machine involves the measurement of the skin temperature of a hand or foot. The 'read out' may be displayed on a screen, or given as a sound signal. As the users learn what to do to increase the temperature, they will effectively be relaxing the muscles of the limb (since this is what causes the flow of blood to increase, and the temperature to rise). This particular method has been used successfully in helping sufferers to 'switch off' headaches at their outset. General relaxation of the area is certainly achieved, but it is not certain that there is full body relaxation. The control of blood pressure and heart rate can be achieved in a similar way, through mental effort.

What is not certain is whether, in the long-term, the person, having 'learned' to achieve the desired result whilst attached to the biofeedback equipment, can continue to do so in everyday life when not 'plugged in'. Other systems, such as meditation and relaxation techniques, do have the ability to influence everyday experience, as well as allowing the possibility of increased 'awareness' and personality development. Biofeedback cannot, as yet, make similar claims.

The best results with biofeedback have been achieved when such methods are combined with meditation and relaxation exercises. Certainly, no biofeedback methods which monitor specific organs or functions should be used without supervision if an attempt is being made to modify an existing health problem.

The more advanced biofeedback methods monitor the brainwave patterns. A very expensive piece of technology, known as the 'mind mirror', displays twelve rows of information, analysing the subject's brain rhythms from both sides of the brain simultaneously. Different patterns of meditation and levels of relaxation can be monitored in this way, and this is certain to be of great value as an aid to stress reduction, if its prohibitive cost can be trimmed sufficiently to make it generally available.

Many hospitals and clinics now utilize biofeedback methods, and anyone with stress problems might suggest to their doctor that this would be a useful method for controlling their symptoms.

Eeman's Relaxation Circuits

An amazing piece of research into the curative properties of human radiations was carried out by the late L.E. Eeman. His work was ahead of its time, and those interested may investigate further by reading his books *Co-operative Healing* (Muller, 1947) and *The Technique of Conscious Evolution* (C.W. Daniel, 1956). In so far as it involves a person attempting to reduce stress and induce relaxation it is worth looking at briefly. The method is completely safe and, in my own experience, frequently effective.

First, Eeman states that the human body has specific electrical polarities. By repeatedly using the methods described, as well as many far more complex ones, and by meticulously recording the results, Eeman came to the conclusion that: 'forces latent in man . . . make the nervous system behave as though there were electromagnetic opposition between its top and its bottom, its right and its left sides, and its front and back, and as though, on all three planes or axes, there were a gradient of potential between extreme polar opposites.'

Eeman found that by linking different aspects of these polarities in various ways he could establish a 'relaxation circuit'. He is careful to state that although, for convenience, he has named certain areas as positive and others as negative, the reverse is equally likely to be correct. Indeed, he makes it clear that whilst the observed phenomenon suggests an electrical analogy, and therefore terminology, in fact it appears to have more to do with short-wave radiation, or magnetic fields, since direct contact with the skin of the area was unnecessary and did not affect the results.

His working hypothesis was 'that conducted wireless radiations emitted by the human body can be used therapeutically, provided that polar opposites are linked by electrical conductors.' His classical diagram of human polarities shows the following characteristics:

Positive: Right foot, right hand, left side of head, top of sternum (breastbone) and base of neck area.
Negative: Left foot, left hand, right side of head and base of spine.

Eeman placed the patient on two copper gauze mats, one under the head and one under the sacrum, and then linked the upper one, by means of a length of copper wire, to the left hand (positive to negative), and the lower one, by similar means, to the right hand (negative to positive).

Ankles were kept in a crossed position.

Eeman emphasizes that the method should only be used on a relaxed subject. (It is strongly recommended that anyone wishing to promote the deep relaxation and sense of well-being that this method usually brings, should first learn to relax by using one or other of the methods described in Chapter 7.)

Eeman states categorically that 'in the absence of voluntary muscular relaxation, reactions may not only be obscured, but frequently reversed'. If a relaxation state is already being achieved, then the use of the 'relaxation circuit' will be found to be most advantageous. Ten minutes is suggested as the minimum, and thirty minutes is the ideal amount of time to spend on this method.

Eeman went on to link, in circuit, ever-increasing numbers of people at the same time. The therapeutic and relaxation effects thus produced are worthy of further research by healing professions. In using the simple circuit described above, nothing but good can result if you are (a) relaxed at the outset, and (b) practise the method for ten to thirty minutes per session, at frequent intervals (several times weekly).

If, rather than sensing progressive warmth, muscular relaxation, well-being and drowsiness, you sense restlessness and discomfort, then the polarities should be reversed, i.e. the left-hand should hold the lead connected to your spine, and the right hand the lead connected to your head. Eeman states that in 25 years of testing many thousands of people he came across no more than half a dozen such 'wrong' reactions, and that even these returned to the normal relaxation circuit after three or four sessions on the otherwise 'tension inducing' circuit. No artificial energy is used in this method, and nothing should be done to connect any part of the simple apparatus with any source of electricity. All that is being done is to place patients in an 'electrical' or 'magnetic' circuit with themselves, in a way which benefits them.

Tapes and Teachers

There are literally hundreds of relaxation and meditation induction tapes on the market. Most of them take the listener verbally through the various stages of relaxation and the majority are useful and effective. Some may not succeed because the voice on the tape may irritate the listener. In many cases, the most successful voice to listen to is your own, and a number of books exist from which you can read appropriate commentaries to aid this. Some tapes consist more of sounds and 'mood' music which enhance the relaxation state. Specific recommendations cannot be given, except to say that most people find these tapes helpful. The following sample induction commentaries may be recorded onto tape and played whenever necessary.

Sample Relaxation Sequence 1

(*To be spoken* slowly *into a tape recorder.*)
   Sit in a comfortable chair, keeping your spine straight.
   'I am sitting comfortably. My eyes are open but I shall be focusing on what takes place inside me. I am at peace with myself, safe and unhurried. My eyes are rolling upwards. My vision is blurred and out of focus. I can feel some strain in the muscles of my eyes. (*Pause to experience this.*) I am looking upwards as far as I can. I can see my eyebrows. The strain is getting stronger. (*Pause.*) I will keep looking upwards. When I blink it feels good.
   If I close my eyes, the strain will ease. I am still looking upwards at my eyebrows. The strain is very strong. (*Pause to experience this.*) I am closing my eyes. The ease and relaxation in the eye muscles is wonderful. The darkness of having my eyes closed is nice. The relaxation and release makes me feel good. This feeling of ease is spreading from my eyes, to my face, and neck and spine. (*Pause to experience*

this.) I feel a general easing and relaxing spreading through my body. (*Pause.*) My neck feels limp and supple. (*Pause.*) My shoulders and arms are at ease and there is a heaviness spreading down my arms. (*Pause to sense the heaviness. Repeat the phrase and pause again.*)

As I breathe in and out I feel I am more and more at ease. As I breathe in, the air brings with it health and energy. As I breathe out, I am aware of letting go, of becoming heavier. Each time I breathe out I feel heavier and more relaxed. I feel like taking a few deep breaths. As I breathe out I feel I am sinking into the chair. (*Pause and repeat.*) My body is becoming heavier and I am sinking deeper. (*Repeat and pause.*) My body feels relaxed and heavy. (*Pause to sense the heaviness, repeat the phrase and pause again.*) My limbs are loose and limp and heavy. (*Pause to sense this and then repeat the phrase.*) I feel safe and at one with myself. I feel at peace with life and totally relaxed. My limbs are heavy. (*Pause and repeat.*) My whole body is heavy. (*Pause and repeat.*) I feel warmth spreading throughout me. (*Pause to experience this, repeat the phrase and pause again.*) I am heavy and warm and safe. (*Pause to enjoy this, then repeat the phrase.*)'

After a short while in this rested state, the following sequence should be listened to. Allow a minute or two of silence on the tape and then record:

'I am going to breathe deeply now. As I breathe in I feel energy and strength coming into my body. (*Repeat several times.*) I feel alert and content. I feel I want to stretch my muscles (*do so*), and my whole body (*do so*). I am opening my eyes and I feel refreshed and alert and relaxed.'

Although this should take about ten minutes, phrases can be repeated as many times as you feel you want to in order to enhance particular feelings of warmth, heaviness, etc. Pauses should be kept for at least ten and up to twenty seconds to sense and savour particular feelings. If wanted, the following sequence can follow on from the relaxation stage after the phrase 'I am heavy and warm and safe' and before commencing the return to wakeful alertness;

alternatively, it can be used at a different time after a short introductory relaxation breathing exercise.

Sample Relaxation Sequence 2

You will be sitting as before and after five to ten cycles of complete breathing, in which you have consciously allowed yourself to release all muscular tension of which you are aware, play a recording of the following (remembering to speak slowly):

'I feel warm, relaxed and safe. (*Repeat several times.*) I feel at peace with myself. I am descending slowly down a spiral staircase. I am going down, deeper and deeper down. I am looking down at the thick carpeting on the stairs which take me down and down and down. I feel comfortable and at ease as I go down the stairs. I feel warm and safe. I am going deeper and deeper, down and down. The peacefulness and quiet is wonderful. I love the quiet and peace. (*Pause.*) I feel safe and at ease as I descend down the carpeted stairs. I feel warm, safe and relaxed. (*Pause.*) I am near the bottom of the stairs and there is a doorway. I see the warm sunshine outside. I step into the golden glow of the sun and feel its embracing warmth. (*Pause.*) I am walking across a meadow in the warm sunshine. I feel happy and safe. This is a beautiful place. I hear birds. (*Pause.*) I see flowers. (*Pause.*) I smell grass. (*Pause.*) There is a river. By the river there is a rowing boat. I am lying in the boat and it is drifting gently on the river. The boat rocks gently as it drifts down the river. I feel safe. The sun is warm on me. The boat is drifting gently down the river. (*Pause.*) I am completely relaxed and at peace. (*Pause.*) I hear the water gently lapping. I feel the warm sun. I am at peace and safe and happy. (*Pause.*) The boat is drifting gently towards the bank of the river. I feel safe and at peace and fully relaxed. I feel safe and at peace and fully relaxed. The boat is gently rocking by the river bank. I step out of it and lie in the shade of a lovely tree. I am completely relaxed and happy and safe. (*Pause.*) This is a beautiful place and wonderful experience. I am warm and relaxed. (*Pause for a minute to experience the peace, silence and relaxed state.*) It is time to go. I shall breathe deeply and open my eyes and be alert and refreshed.'

This sequence can also take about ten minutes and may be used instead of, or as well as, those in the accompanying chapters.

Teachers

Teachers of relaxation and meditation methods can help in instructing the beginner. The Transcendental Meditation system has much to commend it, and it has the virtue of providing introductory courses for beginners as well as follow-up sessions to check on progress.

As far as stress-proofing is concerned, I would emphasize that meditation alone is not enough. It is certainly beneficial, and often dramatically effective in stress reduction but, by now, the reader should be aware that a more extensive programme is needed, as well as meditation.

Massage

Massage therapy, when correctly applied, has been shown to have a profoundly beneficial effect on tension/anxiety levels, reducing feelings of dejection and depression, anger, hostility, confusion and fatigue. This is true of good massage, and finding a good massage therapist can itself by a stressful venture. Once found, it is suggested that regular bodywork be used.

Massage delivered by friends and family can be relaxing,

and a number of books exist which explain the basic methods involved. Many different forms of massage exist, and those which are most recommended are traditional Swedish massage, Shiatsu (Japanese acupressure) and Neuromuscular Technique.

CHAPTER 9

Meditation

There are many forms of meditation, and some will suit one person more than another. It is therefore suggested that each method in this section be tried on a number of consecutive occasions, in order to fully assess its effect on you. Purists, and those who see meditation only in terms of spiritual development, would frown on this advice. There is the story of the pupil who had tried a variety of meditation methods and who, on approaching yet another teacher for advice, was told to lift a glass vial containing layers of coloured sand. Having shaken it as he was instructed, thus mixing all the layers into a grey mass, the teacher admonished him, saying: 'This is the effect on you of all these teachings. Each of them in their own way is pure, but look what has become of them inside you.'

In my experience, when using meditation in an attempt to reduce the effects of stress, some systems are better suited to particular personalities than others. The only way to discover what suits you is to try several methods and judge for yourself – or go to a teacher for guidance. Relaxation methods, as outlined in previous chapters, should have been practised for some weeks before starting to introduce meditation methods. There are a variety of ways of doing this:

1. Continue with the relaxation exercises twice daily and add one meditation session at a suitable time.
2. Replace one of the relaxation exercise with one of the meditation methods.
3. Do a short relaxation exercise, say for five minutes, followed by ten minutes of meditation, twice daily.

Whichever you choose, try to stick to the same meditation method for a week or so to assess whether it enables you to achieve the calmer, more alert state which is intended. What all meditation methods have in common is the conscious attempt to focus the mind on one object. In this respect, the relaxation methods already outlined could be seen as forms of meditation.

The 'pure' meditation that it is hoped you will be able to add to one of the relaxation methods, provides a different dimension to the programme; for, whilst it is not too difficult to concentrate one's attention on the breathing mechanism and on counting whilst breathing, for example, it requires a greater degree of application to concentrate on an abstract thought or image. What is essential in meditation is a device through which the conscious mind can be diverted from everyday thought processes. In separating the relaxation exercises from meditation methods, I am aware that they do overlap. However, whilst meditation leads inevitably to relaxation and perhaps to spiritual awareness, relaxation exercises can seldom lead to more than just relaxation, which is what we are seeking at this stage.

The Distracting Object

The device or 'distracting object' can be a mental picture or image, a word, a sound, a real object, an idea, an activity, or indeed anything. Whatever it is, all other thoughts must thereby be excluded from conscious awareness. There is a form of meditation in which no particular object is selected, but in which the participant attempts to focus on everything that is happening around them, becoming as fully aware of their internal and external environment as possible during the meditation. This has been called 'open meditation'.

All meditation involves a suspension of judgement. The object is observed non-critically. No thoughts about it are encouraged, simply a passive attention to the object. Some methods attempt to combine the use of an object (say breathing or a sound) and the 'open' pattern of meditation in which thoughts entering the mind are 'watched' but not 'judged' and are then replaced by the meditative object.

Research has shown that a variety of physiological changes take place during meditation. Certainly, tension and stress are reduced in the process. Frequently, behaviour patterns involving addiction, such as smoking, overeating and drug or alcohol consumption are improved or controlled by meditation. Such stress-induced conditions as high blood pressure are also markedly affected for the better by the application of successful meditation methods.

In general terms, meditation has been found to produce feelings of greater alertness and ability to concentrate, of being more perceptive, and so on. Many people experience an 'awakening' or a heightening of spiritual awareness. Supporters of these methods often use such phrases as 'cosmic consciousness' and 'transcendental experiences'. These phrases should not put off the would-be meditator for, at the very least, a greater sense of well-being and more relaxed state should follow meditation. If any of the other benefits or experiences also follow, they should be taken as a bonus. Reduction in stress is difficult to measure. Frequently the gradual beneficial changes that do accrue are only measurable by comparison with the previous state of tension. Keeping a record of your results in the stress-assessment lists in Chapter 5 will enable you to make such a comparison after some months of regular relaxation and meditation.

Meditating Posture

The position or posture adopted for meditation is of importance. The classical poses range from the lotus position to the kneeling at prayer position. Most variations insist that during meditation your spine be kept straight, and this should be remembered, whether you decide to sit or kneel (perhaps using a small meditation stool), or even stand.

Many systems and teachers have linked the way we hold and use our bodies with our emotional state. There seems to be a two-way influence, in as much as a physical symptom will usually develop in response to emotional stress, and emotions will be influenced by any tension or 'armouring' in the musculature.

Once the appropriate posture has been adopted, the mind should accept, initially, that you will stay immobile until the completion of the exercise. This stillness is an essential part of meditation and does itself lead to desirable physiological changes, as well as having positive psychological benefits such as increased self-respect and confidence. The self-discipline involved in immobility is enhanced if, during meditation, any irritant such as the buzzing of a fly or an aching of the limbs can be ignored or dismissed and the meditation process continued.

It is known that the meditation experience increases with repetition. Regular meditation requires an element of self-discipline and organization. It is well worth the effort, and once it becomes a part of the daily routine, the oasis of calm and regeneration, which the meditation period brings, will be eagerly anticipated.

Choose a suitably unhurried part of the day to practise. Morning and evening seem to suit most people. Avoid meditating soon after meals, if possible. Adopt a sitting or kneeling position (lying is not suggested for meditation), and remember to keep your spine straight.

Method 1: Concentration

The simplest, and probably the oldest, form of meditation involves concentrating on one object. It has long been established that by allowing your eyes to roll upwards as you begin meditation, the effect is more speedily achieved. Your head should be erect and your eyes should look upwards as far as they can (towards your eyebrows). This may be accompanied by mild muscular discomfort, but this should pass. If this is not found to enhance any of the following methods, then close your eyes from the beginning. Normally, after a short while of maintaining the strained upward-rolled position of the eyes it comes as a relief and a relaxing experience to gently close your eyes and to then continue the method with your eyes closed.

Breathing in a relaxed, unforced manner, focus your mind on an *imagined* object (a cross, a candle flame, a circle of light, or anything else of your choice) or, with your eyes looking ahead, focus on an actual object of a similar nature. Alternatively, with your eyes gently closed or rolled upwards, repeat a meaningless sound in your mind (not out loud).

When you are visualizing an imaginary object, or gazing at a real object, simply dwell passively on it. Thoughts that intrude should be gently discarded and replaced by the image of the object on which you are concentrating. If a sound is being used ('om' or 'aaah', for instance) this should be repeated rhythmically over and over again. It may take on its own rhythm, becoming a continuous drone. The most important point is that concentration should be held on the sound and not directed towards anything else.

Concentrative forms of meditation require persistent practice before they can be maintained for any length of time. At first, the beginner may find that it is not possible to maintain concentration on an image or object (imagined or real) for more than a few seconds at a time before thoughts intrude. Gradually, with patience and discipline, it will be found that minutes at a time will pass in this state and, finally, that it is possible to maintain concentration for as long as is needed. This method, by focusing your mind, enhances relaxation, reduces anxiety, and frequently helps in the elimination of psychosomatic ailments.

One example of concentrative meditation is a Hindu method known as *tratak*. The object of concentration in this method is a burning flame, which is placed at eye level about a foot in front of the meditator. Breathing should be slow, deep and silent. You gaze into the centre of the flame until tears begin to flow, at which point your eyes should be closed, and the image of the flame is then visualized until it vanishes.

Another concentrative meditation is that used by raj yogi. They meditate with their eyes closed, focusing attention on the tip of the nose, or the back of the skull. Experiments on meditators who use these methods showed that very soon after starting meditation, alpha waves (a sign of a relaxed state) appeared, and that these were maintained without interruption, despite the following external stimuli being administered: loud banging noises; the meditator's hands being placed in cold water or being touched with a hot tube; bright light; vibration from a tuning fork etc. In other words, the meditation process was so powerful that none of these stimuli could disturb it or its relaxing effect (as measured by alpha brain wave patterns).

When effectively performed, meditation which makes use of concentration, blots out all other sensations and thoughts. This is the key to its usefulness in stress-proofing, for with practice it becomes possible to focus the mind on one thing, be it a sound or an object, and detach oneself from all others.

A few minutes in this silent state has restorative and relaxing effects. It is suggested that an attempt is made to spend ten minutes at a time performing such exercises, but that at first only a few minutes be attempted, perhaps tagged on to the end of a relaxation method.

Method 2: Contemplation

In many ways this method is similar to the previous one. The object in the mind of the meditator can be an abstract idea, such as 'goodness', 'love', 'truth', etc. or the idea of God. Extension of this can be to use repetitive sounds or phrases, which are repeated rhythmically and silently. For example: 'God is love' or 'Hail Mary full of Grace, the Lord is with thee', etc. Any meaningful phrase will do. As long as the repeated phrase occupies your mind totally, it will have its effect.

The constant barrage of thoughts and images, most of them meaningless and useless, that usually occupy our minds, needs to be stilled, and these methods are designed to achieve this. A person's view of the world and of themself may well be altered as a result, sometimes for only a short time and sometimes permanently.

For those who would rather avoid religious connotations during meditation, the suggestion of Krishnamurti, the Indian philosopher, is that the sound to be repeated could well be 'coca-cola, coca-cola'. There is certainly no reason why this should not be as effective as any other object or sound in silencing thought. There are those, though, who maintain that the content and vibrational quality of the 'mantra', or repeated words or sounds, determines their effect. However, research has tended to support the idea that it is the act of repetition and not the actual sound that produces the desired result, at least in so far as relaxation is concerned.

Herbert Benson MD, author of *Relaxation Response*, says that the repeated word 'bananas' will do the trick. This, of course, may be seen as an affront to the spiritual connotations of meditating, but in so far as it is our concern to achieve relaxation, 'bananas' or 'coca-cola' would do as well as anything else.

After ten minutes of this, allow your mind to become aware of your surroundings and how you feel, and then open your eyes, stretch your body and return to normal activities.

Method 3: Meditating on 'Bubbles' of Thought

Adopt the desired position, and induce a state of relaxation. See your mind as the surface of a pond – smooth and calm. Thoughts that enter your mind should be seen as bubbles rising from the depths of the pond. They should be observed, not pursued. In other words, the deliberate following of the thought process is avoided. Simply *detach* yourself and observe your thoughts as they 'bubble' to the surface. Take note of the thought and then gently, without any force, return to your contemplation of the smooth surface of the pond.

It is also possible to sink under the surface of the pond, into deeper layers of consciousness as time goes by. As long as thoughts are not intrusive, but are observed and then depart, just like the bubbles, the meditation process is continuing. After ten minutes or so, allow your mind to focus on your immediate environment; sense a degree of relaxation and then end the session.

Method 4: Meditating on Your Corner of Heaven

In this method, after adopting an initial posture, and relaxing consciously, with your eyes closed or rolled upwards, begin to visualize a place in which you would feel happy and safe. This could be a real, remembered place. It could be a room or a country or garden scene, or any other place to which you could go whenever you wanted peace and a feeling of security.

This place should be so visualized (imagined in your mind's eye) that it can be stepped into and out of as time goes by. If it is a room, then furnishings can be changed, rearranged or added to. Colours should be seen and, if possible, all your senses should gradually be brought into the meditation. Try to hear the sounds (for example, clocks ticking, birds singing etc.); smell the various smells (a log fire, newly mown grass, flowers); feel the textures (bark of the tree, velvet upholstery), and so on. There is no limit to the degree of embroidery that is possible in creating this special place.

All the powers of your imagination should be employed. This sort of meditation has been called 'creating a safe harbour', and it should be seen by the meditator, whilst conscious of its imagined nature, to be useful as a retreat whenever it is needed. It is a meditation which uses all the senses, and is suitable for many who find it too difficult a task to maintain concentration on one object. After ten minutes or so, you should step out of the picture and return to your normal environment, knowing that the 'safe place' remains untouched and ready for the next visit.

Whichever method of meditation suits you best, it is suggested that you construct such a 'safe haven' for yourself anyway, as it is a valuable exercise in imagery, and is of great use in visualization techniques (see the next chapter).

Method 5: Breathing and Colour Visualization

Adopt a reclining or sitting position of comfort in an appropriate room. Breathe deeply several times, and sense a feeling of safe, warm ease. Continue to breathe slowly and deeply, but not in a straining manner. As you breathe, visualize the colours red, orange and yellow flowing upwards into your solar plexus. These hues should be visualized one at a time and seen as rivers of colour. The breathing rhythm should not be controlled, but should be allowed to find its own pace and depth.

The colours should be seen to flow at a steady, unhurried pace. After spending a minute or so on each of the first three colours, visualize the colour green flowing into your solar plexus from directly in front of you. Spend a minute or so breathing in a slow, rhythmic manner with the image of a river of green light entering your body.

Follow this with blue, indigo and violet, one at a time; these should be seen as being breathed inwards from the air above you. Again, spend a minute or so visualizing each of these colours. The only problem presented by this method is the difficulty some people have in visualizing colours. This becomes easier with practice, although some colours will be easier to 'see' than others.

After completing the colour spectrum, see yourself as being bathed in blue light, and end the meditation with a deep sense of peace and calm before opening your eyes and resuming normal activities.

Method 6: Tactile Meditation

This method uses the sense of touch to help procure the meditative state. The requirements are either a set of 'worry beads' or four or five pebbles. Adopt a relaxed posture, keeping your spine straight, and consciously 'let go' of any muscular tensions. Hold the beads gently in one hand and, with the other, rhythmically and methodically move them between your fingers, touching them one at a time.

As each bead is moved, it should be felt and counted. It is helpful to have a slow, rhythmical count, up to about five. This is then repeated over and over. Count, handle and 'hear' the beads – one, two, three, four, five. The same effect can be achieved by passing pebbles from one hand to the other. Feel, sense and count them, focusing all your attention on this slow, repetitive movement.

After ten minutes, open your eyes and resume your normal activities.

Method 7: Attention to Life

This is not a method to be used at the daily or twice-daily relaxation-meditation sessions, but rather during normal activities. The objective is to consciously focus all your attention on the particular moment, activity or task. If a mundane activity is selected for this treatment, then a focusing on all aspects of it is required.

Let's take a task such as washing your hands or face. Your eyes should be closed and all your senses used to feel and register everything about this simple act. Such sensations as soap being lathered on wet hands, the feel, sound, smell and temperature changes of the whole procedure, should be focused on and registered as acutely as possible.

Whatever the particular action chosen (and it is a good idea to pick several short actions each day), the effect is to heighten awareness, and to encourage a feeling of being fully in the 'here and now' rather than doing such everyday tasks whilst thinking about other things. In time, it will become possible to concentrate on the present for longer and longer periods.

This type of meditation requires that you first consciously

relax all muscles, apart from those essential to the task, and that only enough muscular effort is used to ensure its successful completion. Whether the task is peeling a piece of fruit or a vegetable, or making a bed, or driving a car, or writing a letter, what is essential is that all the senses be used, and that total application of your mind is to that task alone. All other thoughts and concerns should be ignored.

If you can learn to focus totally on present time, albeit for short periods, you will begin to reduce the amount of stress factors which are constantly at work. You will do whatever you have to do more efficiently, with greater satisfaction and less effort. This is one of the values of a truly absorbing hobby, be it music, painting, gardening or anything else – it is so beneficial in terms of reducing stress.

Note: All meditation methods will assist in achieving relaxation. Indeed, meditation is not possible without it. There is no right or wrong way of meditating, as long as the conscious mind is being stilled. If you come across any difficulties, take advice from a teacher of these methods.

CHAPTER 10

Using the Power of
Your Mind for Healing

There is overwhelming evidence that much of the illness suffered by mankind results to some extent from stress and emotional causes. The evidence that such illness can be reversed by means of a shift in a person's psychological make-up is becoming equally overwhelming. Such means of stimulating the self-healing process involve believing that you can be better; seeing yourself getting better; visualizing, in ways that make sense to yourself, the actual disease process being overcome by your body.

The Simontons, in their excellent book *Getting Well Again* (Bantam), describe the changes which they have observed in the upward spiral towards recovery. It is as well to realize that their work has dealt mainly with cancer. Even so, they have observed the healing power of the mind operating in many people who have controlled or overcome their disease, and if this is true of cancer, then it can be applied to any reversible health problem, chronic or acute.

First, say the Simontons, it is noticeable that with the diagnosis of a life-threatening disease, the individual appears to gain new perspectives on his or her problems. Further, the threat to life seems to release them from previous behaviour patterns into which they were locked by habit (for example, hostility, long suppressed, can now be expressed). Often, personality changes occur, through which old attitudes and rules of conduct are suspended, and unresolved conflicts show signs of resolution. These changes are accompanied by a lifting of depression and greater psychological energy. It is as though, in these people, the disease has given them permission to change. As hope and a greater desire to live begin to operate, physical changes begin to be felt, and they reinforce the positive changes in the psychological state. Eventually, with recovery, the person often enjoys better health than ever before.

Visualization and Guided Imagery

How can this sort of change be encouraged and enhanced? It is by no means the norm, but is nevertheless seen in many of those patients who did overcome their illness. If such changes could be included in the programme of treatment for all in ill health, what a revolution it would cause. As already mentioned, in order to consciously employ such knowledge to your advantage, you must use your own belief system. In order to do this effectively, a brief outline is necessary of how altered attitudes and the techniques of visualization and 'guided imagery' can reinforce the process.

Psychological stress, resulting in depression and despair, acts through your brain to negatively influence your body's defence and control systems (such as your immune system and hormonal activity) resulting in inadequate protection and breakdown in normal health. In such a case, a variety of other variables, ranging from inherited factors to nutritional and structural factors, will determine just what parts of the body begin to malfunction and become diseased.

The reversal of this process, if it is to be effective, needs to begin on the psychological level, thus influencing the brain centres which determine hormonal and immune system function, and thus the healing process. The simple answer, then, is that hope and anticipation of recovery need to be linked with altered attitudes and reduced anxiety. And, from a holistic viewpoint, all other aspects of health – for instance, diet and exercise – should at this point also be corrected.

The relaxation exercises and simple meditation methods previously explained will have opened the way for further use of the power of your mind in the healing process. The guided imagery or visualization methods which follow, show how to make use of your mind's power. You should vary the images and phrases to suit your own particular needs.

Method 1

Use the relaxation method that most suits you in order, within a few minutes, to induce a sense of ease. This could be a breathing technique or progressive muscular relaxation (see Chapter 8). Use the 'safe haven' meditation (page 189) in order to spend two or three minutes in safe, peaceful and harmonious contemplation.

You are now ready for guided visualization to promote healing. Create in your mind a picture of any illness or ailment you have. This should be done in a way that makes sense to you. It does not have to be scientifically accurate. Suggestions follow on how this might be done.

Having visualized your ailment, try to visualize your body's defence and healing mechanisms overcoming, controlling or correcting the condition. It is as well to keep firmly in mind that there are few, if any, conditions which cannot be improved, controlled or normalized by virtue of the self-healing mechanisms of the body. If any treatment is being undertaken to help the condition, visualize this, too, in whatever way makes sense to you. See your body healing and normalizing the problem with the aid of whatever treatment you are having. Know that you will be well again.

See yourself well, healthy, free of pain or discomfort; visualize yourself being active and doing something pleasant, such as walking in a sunlit meadow or swimming in a warm clear sea. Visualize yourself achieving something you have as a goal in life. Feel satisfied and content that you are, in this way, able to support and participate consciously in your recovery.

When you have completed the visualization, either rest for a while or resume your normal activities. Do this exercise two or three times daily, as well as or instead of your relaxation programme. Five to ten minutes of this imagery should be performed on each occasion.

Here are some suggestions for visualization of illnesses, and how your body and treatment will be able to overcome them:

Painful Area, Joint, Muscle etc. (e.g. arthritis, rheumatism)

See the area and visualize the blood vessels as being congested with dark red blood; see the tense, inflamed muscles and the irritated joint surfaces. Now see fresh, pink, oxygen-rich blood, full of healing white blood cells, flushing through your blood vessels, carrying away the rough deposits, relaxing your tense muscles. Visualize the area again, but this time see it as relaxed, free of congestion and with no crystals, just smooth, polished joint surfaces and healthy pink muscles and blood. See your joints and muscles performing their normal functions, such as running, lifting, bending etc.

An Open Wound or Ulcer

Picture the area and see the raw, inflamed tissues. Visualize the bloodstream gently covering the area with a soothing lining of protective cells. See them proliferating and dividing to form new, healthy tissue. See the wound covered and normal. See yourself well and healthy and free of pain.

A Bronchial Problem

See your lungs and their network of tubes being irritated by mucous deposits. See the mucus being cleared away by your body, and see your air passages clearing and expanding to allow a free passage of air. Visualize the removed debris being easily coughed up, and then picture the soft mucous membrane lining your air passages and producing just enough clear liquid to lubricate the movement of the surfaces. See your lungs expanding to their full capacity. See yourself walking, running or enjoying any activity which at present might be difficult.

Circulatory Problems

See your narrowed blood vessels, and imagine them constricted and perhaps partly obstructed. Visualize your body, aided by any treatment you are undergoing, as dilating your blood vessels, clearing away any obstructions and relaxing the small muscles which contract the vessels. See fresh, healthy blood flushing through your arteries. See areas, normally deprived of blood, as flushed and warm. The detail of how this takes place is irrelevant. What matters is that you see something take place which will lead to the desired state.

The deposits in the blood vessels can be seen as a chalky lining, and their removal can be seen as a melting or chipping away by the body's defence mechanism, represented in your visualization by white blood cells which can be pictured as soldiers or an army of workers. The more graphic and real the images, the better.

In dealing with such serious problems as cancer, these methods are extremely helpful. Some cancer patients learn to visualize the tumour cells as grey, soft masses which are attacked by this white blood cell army and destroyed. The white cells can be pictured as knights on horseback, or soldiers carrying flame throwers, or as woodsmen carrying axes.

Any ailment or condition can be approached this way, and negative thoughts, doubts and fears can thus be overcome. A sense of being in control of the healing process brings with it self-confidence and hope; the will to live, and the determination not to give in. Real physical changes can stem directly from 'guided imagery' of this type. Believing on your recovery makes it all the more likely, and speeds up the process.

It is, though, not possible for everyone to visualize pictures of the sort suggested. Some people just cannot think in this way, and in such cases verbal images or 'feelings' are perfectly adequate. Remember that the exercise is flexible enough to be used by anyone. It is a matter of seeing the problem your way, and imagining the way in which your body, sustained by treatment, may overcome illness.

The images you select, and the meaning that they hold for you, are of importance. In this respect, it is worth emphasizing that:

1. The illness must be seen as a weak, vulnerable enemy;
2. The body's defence capacity must be seen as strong and easily capable of destroying and removing the enemy;
3. Previously damaged areas are thought of as easily

repaired by the body, and should be seen as normal again;

4. Any debris from the healing process is thought of as easily cleared from the body and should be seen as flushed away;

5. Any treatment should be seen as supportive of the powerful healing mechanisms, and providing an even more certain end to the problem.

Method 2

Whereas method 1 is suitable for promoting recovery from, or control of, actual illness, this method is aimed at improving health and function in a person who shows no obvious signs of illness. The aim might be to achieve that extra dimension of health and well-being that most people never reach. Extra vitality and energy might be another aim. A slimmer more supple body might be another.

Initially, therefore, you must have in your mind the ideal state which you seek. Use the relaxation method that most suits you in order, within a few minutes, to induce a sense of ease. This could be a breathing technique or the progressive muscular relaxation exercise (see Chapter 7). Use the 'safe haven' meditation (see page 189) in order to spend two or three minutes in peaceful and harmonious contemplation. You are now ready for a creative visualization exercise.

Visualize or imagine the desired state exactly as you wish it to be. (You are slimmer, more energetic, or your hair is thick and silky, etc.). If it relates to your ability to deal with others, see yourself in a situation which might previously have bothered you, but which you visualize in the exercise as being easily coped with. Everything proceeds easily and smoothly; you are confident and relaxed.

Retain strongly in your mind the image or idea you wish

to promote. To this picture add appropriate affirmative statements (silently or out loud). For example: 'I am slim and supply and healthy'; 'I feel energetic and full of vitality'; 'My body is strong, energetic and well'; 'I am happy and relaxed all the time'.

These or other appropriate affirmations, which you repeat to yourself, are most important since they can have a physiological effect. (Recall the effect on your body of the affirmation 'my arm is getting warmer' in the autogenic training exercise). It is also important that such statements are not of a negative nature. For instance, don't say: 'I no longer feel tired', but say 'I feel wide awake and energetic'. It is also important that the statement sounds right to you, and thus fulfils the role that it should.

After a few minutes of visualizing your desired goal, and then affirming it with positive statements, remind yourself that the goal you seek is the normal and natural state, to which we are all entitled, that the relaxation and visualization method is removing obstacles and blockages which might have been preventing this desired natural state from occurring. In this way you mentally affirm that what you seek is not a wild preposterous dream, but a reasonable and natural expectation.

Vizualize the vital energy of life coursing through, and see it in whatever terms make sense to you. See health as an energy which glows, warm and golden, and which bathes and succours you. Feel its warmth and see its glow as you are surrounded and bathed by this vital force, which your relaxed state is opening you to.

If transient thoughts or negative doubts intrude, just repeat your appropriate affirmation – which you should have decided on in advance – or visualize your desired goal, or see and feel the energy previously described. Continue with this for as long as you wish, but not less than five and not more than twenty minutes is probably a reasonable range of times to be guided by. The various aspects of the exercise can also be repeated as often as you wish.

Needless to say, it is desirable that, in conjunction with such a visualization programme, you actually do things to enhance the likelihood of success, whether this involves eating a balanced diet or getting enough exercise. These visualization techniques are relaxing and health-promoting extensions of the exercises described in the chapters on relaxation and meditation.

By applying, as appropriate, methods 1 and 2, the innate self-healing capacity of your body is allowed to operate. This is not something you can force, but by passive attention to the positive images and ideas employed, you are creating a situation in which the desired outcome becomes more probable.

By altering your attitudes, coming to believe that healing and recovery are going to take place, and by giving your mind and body the chance to accomplish its self-regulating, homoeostatic endeavours, profound changes can occur. The power of the mind, when harnessed to positive goals which are *believed* to be attainable, can transform a sick person to a well one, and a well person to a positively healthy one.

Index

Of further interest . . .

CLEAR BODY
CLEAR MIND

How to be healthy in a polluted world

LEON CHAITOW

Living in an increasingly toxic and stressful world makes unprecedented demands on the human body, mind and spirit. So new is the toxic load we all have to deal with, that even recognizing the symptoms and causes of toxicity is difficult. This eminently practical guide confronts the escalating problems of physical and mental pollution in our daily lives and shows you how to detoxify yourself through self-help techniques.

- Entirely practical

- Full instructions given

- Unique questionnaires

- Complete detoxification programmes

- Breathing, stretching and aerobic exercises
- Diet, massage and hydrotherapy techniques
- Relaxation, meditation and visualization methods